The Harvest of Faith

THE HARVEST OF FAITH

Toward a Better Understanding
between Islam and Judaism

Youssef M. Khakshouri

Edited by Ephraim Davidoff

Translated by Daniel Salaimani

Elliott & Thompson
London

Contents

Preface page 7

Introduction / 9

Chapter One / 11
Co-existence with the Possessors of a
Heavenly Book in the *Gracious Koran*

Chapter Two / 19
Freedom of Thought in Islam.

Chapter Three / 21
Are Those Possessing a Heavenly Book Pure ?

Chapter Four / 25
The Kind Attention of the Almighty God to the
Children of Israel in the *Gracious Koran*.

Chapter Five / 33
Observing the *Holy Koran*: A Warning to the Unbelievers

Chapter Six / 37
Has the *Torah* been Altered?

Chapter Seven / 42
Jerusalem and Palestine

Chapter Eight / 48
Changing of *Kibla*

CONTENTS

Chapter Nine / 53
Jihad

Chapter Ten / 56
God's Angels

Chapter Eleven / 57
Verses of Reprimand

Chapter Twelve / 81
Prophet of Islam and Possessors of a Heavenly Book.

Chapter Thirteen / 101
The Prophet Jesus Christ

Chapter Fourteen / 105
The Imams and the Jews

Chapter Fifteen / 107
Imam Ali's Justice

Chapter Sixteen / 111
Why does Anti-Semitism Exist?

Chapter Seventeen / 117
The Children of Israel Represent a Benefit for All Religions.

Bibliography / 123
About the Author / 125

Preface

My purpose in writing this book is to create a better understanding and unanimity amongst all members of monotheistic faiths – those faiths which possess a heavenly book and are believers in a heavenly faith.Almighty God sent his prophets to guide human beings, to keep them from deviation and misfortune, and to prevent them straying from the path of truth and happiness. Those who believe in the uniqueness of God and the mission of the Divine prophets should choose to stand firm against polytheism, idolatry, fraud, deviation, tyranny, cruelty and crime. They should seek to do their best performing their divine duties, remain alert, and not rely on anyone or anything but the Almighty God. That prejudice, suggestibility, a lack of knowledge and limited religious insight leads some followers to embrace spitefulness, quarrels – even wars – deny God's purposes. No faithful monotheist should ever kill, act dishonourably, destroy, oppress, slander the religious beliefs of others or annihilate anything in the name of their faith. Religion should provide happiness and comfort for people as they lead their lives. It should not invoke separation, quarrels, deceit, or seek to ever oppress the belief of others. This book has been conceived on the basis of the Holy aim of increasing understanding among the followers of Divine religions – the children of Ibrahim. Needless to say, the purpose of the author is to pave a road to cooperation, free negotiation, and offer the possibility of a peaceful life, especially those three great contemporary religions – Islam, Judaism, and Christianity. I have tried to disperse the dark clouds that have always hidden the sunny and pleasant task of seeking good relationships among the followers of Ibrahimian religions. Considering what has too often happened in the past, and still continues to haunt the human race today, my aim will not be easy – but it will not be impossible either.

During the long history of religion, peacemakers, intellectuals and real believers have always suffered from limited mental horizons. Some of the followers of the divine religions lack vital knowledge. Today we should reduce the effects of such hiatus, and seek instead to promote friendship, peace, cooperation and progress. If this book will assist in taking even a small step towards this I will have reached my goal. I have always wondered why there are such quarrels and hostility among the followers of monotheistic religions, when we all worship the same single God.

By necessity, I have had to draw on the works of great writers and learned sages. My motivation is an ardent desire to see the followers of the monotheistic religions living together in peace and well-being. I have endeavored to focus on positive historical events, and have refrained from referring to unpleasant and unwholesome incidents. I wish to prevent divisiveness and hostility.

Preface

My hope is that the book will contribute, in some way, to the creation of greater understanding and peace between nations.

Youssef M. Khakshouri

INTRODUCTION

Peace and Unity

On 19th November 1977 Anwar Sadat, the President of Egypt said, in a speech to the Israeli Parliament:

I have come here today to open a new chapter in the relationship between Israel and Egypt and lay the foundation of peace. We – the Jews, the Moslems and the Christians – all love this Holy Land, worship the same single God, and believe that the Divine commands are issued on the basis of love, kindness, sincerity, security and peace.
'Everyone who loses his life is a human being, no matter if he be Jewish or Arab. Every woman who becomes a widow is also a human being, deserving a happy life, no matter whether she is Arab or Jewish. The innocent children who lose their parents are all our children needing parental love, no matter whether they live in Israel or in Arab countries. I have come here in order to establish a durable and just peace together, so that in the future there will not be any bloodshed. To reach this aim I am ready to travel to the farthest place of the world.

The establishment of peace between France and Germany after the Second World War was one of the most interesting historical events of the last century. The peace between these two nations was fashioned after centuries of hostility and spitefulness. It caused the animosities of the past to be forgotten, and gave place to peaceful cooperation and the establishment of European unity. Although there are still some local unresolved problems between various European peoples, nobody believes that another major European war will ever happen again.
Since we are living in a time when many people are aware of the horrible consequences of war and appreciate peace and a life without fear, it is surely not a rash prediction to say that peace should prevail all over the world. In fact, many beings on this earth feel peace is the necessity of our age, and, in my opinion, we are not far from achieving such an aspiration.
The unity of Nature is not damaged by the variety of natural elements, and cultural and national differences should not prevent the unity of the human race. According to the *Holy Koran*, the variety of languages and ideas is a sign of divinity, since it leads to a better understanding. Knowing about different civilizations should have the same effect. The roots of disagreement derive from lack of mutual understanding, and from being unaware of the thoughts of others. I fondly hope that brotherhood and sincerity among human beings,

especially among those followers of the Divine religions, form the basic principle of human relations. In this way negotiations, cooperation, and unanimity can be substituted for difference and hostility.

May the Almighty God help us know each other free from lies and prejudice. That we sheathe our swords of hate and stretch out our hands in friendship and peace. It is worth repeating that the true source of hostility and hate are often found in our lack of knowledge about each other's faiths. All too often, we have wrong or partial information, much of it untrue or based on rumour and prejudice. This state of affairs has separated human societies from each other for too long.

Chapter One

•

Co-existence with the Possessors of a Heavenly Book in the *Gracious Koran*

I believe the creation of understanding and friendship amongst members of the monotheistic faiths who possess a heavenly book is in compliance with the commands of the Almighty God. They appear in the *Holy Koran* in the form of verses sent to His prophet. I, Youssef Khakshouri, a Jew from Orumia in Iran, also believe Mohammed to be a true messenger of the Almighty God, and the *Gracious Koran* to be his Holy Book. I have always had the good fortune to enjoy the friendship and brotherhood of my Moslem compatriots, but I have found that sometimes misinterpretation of the verses and sayings about the believers of other religions have unfortunately created a separation between many Jews and Moslems, leading to displays of contempt towards each other.

With this in mind, I decided to examine and analyze the verses dealing with the Children of Israel and some other believers that are contained in the *Gracious Koran*. For this purpose I studied the translation of the Holy Book repeatedly, hoping to discover among its 6,219 verses some that advocate the idea of understanding and friendship which would remove the present misunderstandings. It is worth mentioning that about seven hundred verses in the *Gracious Koran* (around ten per cent of the Holy text) refer to the Children of Israel and their prophets. Moslems respect the sanctity of the Jews and also believe their prophets to be the messengers of God. This fact in itself is a good reason for seeking the prevalence of peace and understanding among each religion's followers.

Heavenly Religions Save Human Beings

One point which these three heavenly faiths have in common is their belief in the coming of the 'end of the world', when by the mercy of the Almighty God, wolves and lambs will live together peacefully. Why should we not try to aspire towards this holy aim?

Behaving Moderately Towards the Followers of a Heavenly Book

Hereafter I will specify some verses from the *Gracious Koran* which advocate moderate behaviour towards the followers of a heavenly book in general, and towards the Children of Israel specifically:

CO-EXISTENCE WITH THE POSSESSORS OF A HEAVENLY BOOK...

There is no compulsion in religion; truly the right way has become clearly distinct from error; therefore, whoever disbelieves in the Shaitan and believes in Allah, he indeed has laid hold on the firmest handle, which shall not break off, and Allah is Hearing, Knowing.

لَا إِكْرَاهَ فِى ٱلدِّينِ قَد تَّبَيَّنَ ٱلرُّشْدُ مِنَ ٱلْغَىِّ فَمَن يَكْفُرْ بِٱلطَّاغُوتِ وَيُؤْمِنۢ بِٱللَّهِ فَقَدِ ٱسْتَمْسَكَ بِٱلْعُرْوَةِ ٱلْوُثْقَىٰ لَا ٱنفِصَامَ لَهَا وَٱللَّهُ سَمِيعٌ عَلِيمٌ ۝

Baqarah 256

At the end of the *Sura Al-Maidah 8*, we read:

O you who believe! Be upright for Allah, bearers of witness with justice, and let not hatred of a people incite you not to act equitably; act equitably, that is nearer to piety, and be careful of (your duty to) Allah; surely Allah is Aware of what you do.

يَٰٓأَيُّهَا ٱلَّذِينَ ءَامَنُوا۟ كُونُوا۟ قَوَّٰمِينَ لِلَّهِ شُهَدَآءَ بِٱلْقِسْطِ وَلَا يَجْرِمَنَّكُمْ شَنَـَٔانُ قَوْمٍ عَلَىٰٓ أَلَّا تَعْدِلُوا۟ ٱعْدِلُوا۟ هُوَ أَقْرَبُ لِلتَّقْوَىٰ وَٱتَّقُوا۟ ٱللَّهَ إِنَّ ٱللَّهَ خَبِيرٌۢ بِمَا تَعْمَلُونَ ۝

In *Sura Al-Jasiyah 16*, we read:

And certainly We gave the Book and the wisdom and the prophecy to the children of Israel, and We gave them of the goodly things, and We made them excel the nations.

وَلَقَدْ ءَاتَيْنَا بَنِىٓ إِسْرَٰٓءِيلَ ٱلْكِتَٰبَ وَٱلْحُكْمَ وَٱلنُّبُوَّةَ وَرَزَقْنَٰهُم مِّنَ ٱلطَّيِّبَٰتِ وَفَضَّلْنَٰهُمْ عَلَى ٱلْعَٰلَمِينَ

In *Sura Al-Baqarah 58* we read:

And when We said: Enter this city, then eat from it a plenteous (food) wherever you wish, and enter the gate making obeisance, and say, forgiveness. We will forgive you your wrongs and give more to those who do good (to others).

وَإِذْ قُلْنَا ٱدْخُلُوا۟ هَٰذِهِ ٱلْقَرْيَةَ فَكُلُوا۟ مِنْهَا حَيْثُ شِئْتُمْ رَغَدًا وَٱدْخُلُوا۟ ٱلْبَابَ سُجَّدًا وَقُولُوا۟ حِطَّةٌ نَّغْفِرْ لَكُمْ خَطَٰيَٰكُمْ وَسَنَزِيدُ ٱلْمُحْسِنِينَ ۝

It is clearly necessary to begin to know each other better, and to clear minds from both sides. Based on this idea, I will show that the conflicts and altercations between the two sides are baseless and devoid of sense. In the *Gracious Koran*, the Children of Israel are treated with respect. (It is worth mentioning here that one of the hundred and fourteen *Suras* in the *Gracious Koran – Sura 17: Al-Osara* – is named after the Children of Israel.) With the spreading of Islam and the expansion of the Prophet Mohammed's mission, we do find some verses in the *Gracious Koran* directed against sinners and stubborn people who only understand their own ways of thought. The purpose of these rebukes is to draw attention to those sinners. They offended the Prophet Mohammed, causing him to be dissatisfied and unhappy about their deeds and their ways of behaving.

This displeasure appears in some verses of the *Gracious Koran*. Indeed, on some occasions, the Almighty God consoles his true prophet – *Sura Yunus 99*.

CHAPTER ONE

It should be mentioned that many of the Children of Israel also hated their own sinners. It could be said the relevant verses in the *Gracious Koran* show the kindness of the Almighty God to all pious Jews. When the Prophet Mohammed took offense at the actions of some Jewish sinners, and as a result some condemnatory verses were sent, it simply shows once more how much the religion of Islam respects Jewish believers and the nation of Israel. I should also mention that all religions, especially those that possess a heavenly book, are based on common values; consequently, minor differences in ideas and taste should not be considered as weakening this common basis.

In view of this, does it make sense that people quarrel and argue about trivial variations in beliefs, and thus misuse religion, so that instead of bringing happiness to human beings it becomes a instrument of violence and spite? Is it appropriate to kill, torture, and exploit in the name of religion?

There can be no doubt that we all follow the precept of the Ibrahimian religion – a precept basic to all three religions – that even more than respect for ownership, the respect for human life is paramount. Murder is forbidden. Surely this is common reason enough for any unification of belief. The *Sura Al-Imran 64* that was sent by the Almighty God to his gracious Prophet 1,400 years ago is, in fact, a proposal for peace among all human beings. Is it not very regrettable and sad that this proposal is ignored by the believers of the heavenly religions, including the Moslems? As stability and peaceful coexistence is the ideal of every human being, it is incumbent upon all of us to help peoples and nations to reach such ideals. The importance of cooperation, unity and understanding amongst the peoples of the world is clear to everyone. Only in this way it is possible to endeavor to develop a better life for all and the solving of our common problems. Co-operation on an international level is the best and most effective way to solve problems, and prevent the violence and wars which are so harmful to us all.

Effective communication via the modern media, combined with the possibility which now exists for many people to travel anywhere will create chances to visit and communicate with people of different colour, race, ideas and religion. We could all co-operate to achieve peace and prosperity.

**Teachings of the *Gracious Koran*
Concerning Unity Among Heavenly Religions**

In order to know about the teachings of the *Gracious Koran* on this matter, I mention some relevant verses:

If you do good openly or do it in secret or pardon an evil, then surely Allah is Pardoning, Powerful.

إِنْ تُبْدُوا خَيْرًا أَوْ تُخْفُوهُ أَوْ تَعْفُوا عَنْ سُوءٍ
فَإِنَّ اللَّهَ كَانَ عَفُوًّا قَدِيرًا

Al-Nisa 149

CO-EXISTENCE WITH THE POSSESSORS OF A HEAVENLY BOOK...

Surely those who believe and those who are Jews and the Sebeans and the Christians whoever believes in Allah and the last day and does good—they shall have no fear nor shall they grieve.

إِنَّ الَّذِينَ آمَنُوا وَالَّذِينَ هَادُوا وَالصَّابِئُونَ وَالنَّصَارَىٰ مَنْ آمَنَ بِاللَّهِ وَالْيَوْمِ الْآخِرِ وَعَمِلَ صَالِحًا فَلَا خَوْفٌ عَلَيْهِمْ وَلَا هُمْ يَحْزَنُونَ ۝

Al-Maidah 69

O people! be careful of (your duty to) your Lord, Who created you from a single being and created its mate of the same (kind) and spread from these two, many men and women; and be careful of (your duty to) Allah, by whom you demand one of another (your rights), and (to) the ties of relationship; surely Allah ever watches over you.

يَا أَيُّهَا النَّاسُ اتَّقُوا رَبَّكُمُ الَّذِي خَلَقَكُم مِّن نَّفْسٍ وَاحِدَةٍ وَخَلَقَ مِنْهَا زَوْجَهَا وَبَثَّ مِنْهُمَا رِجَالًا كَثِيرًا وَنِسَاءً ۚ وَاتَّقُوا اللَّهَ الَّذِي تَسَاءَلُونَ بِهِ وَالْأَرْحَامَ ۚ إِنَّ اللَّهَ كَانَ عَلَيْكُمْ رَقِيبًا

Al-Nisa 1

This day (all) the good things are allowed to you; and the food of those who have been given the Book is lawful for you and your food is lawful for them; and the chaste from among the believing women and the chaste from among those who have been given the Book before you (are lawful for you); when you have given them their dowries, taking (them) in marriage, not fornicating nor taking them for paramours in secret; and whoever denies faith, his work indeed is of no account, and in the hereafter he shall be one of the losers.

الْيَوْمَ أُحِلَّ لَكُمُ الطَّيِّبَاتُ ۖ وَطَعَامُ الَّذِينَ أُوتُوا الْكِتَابَ حِلٌّ لَّكُمْ وَطَعَامُكُمْ حِلٌّ لَّهُمْ ۖ وَالْمُحْصَنَاتُ مِنَ الْمُؤْمِنَاتِ وَالْمُحْصَنَاتُ مِنَ الَّذِينَ أُوتُوا الْكِتَابَ مِن قَبْلِكُمْ إِذَا آتَيْتُمُوهُنَّ أُجُورَهُنَّ مُحْصِنِينَ غَيْرَ مُسَافِحِينَ وَلَا مُتَّخِذِي أَخْدَانٍ ۗ وَمَن يَكْفُرْ بِالْإِيمَانِ فَقَدْ حَبِطَ عَمَلُهُ وَهُوَ فِي الْآخِرَةِ مِنَ الْخَاسِرِينَ

Al-Maidah 5

Say: O followers of the Book! come to an equitable proposition between us and you that we shall not serve any but Allah and (that) we shall not associate aught with Him, and (that) some of us shall not take others for lords besides Allah; but if they turn back, then say: Bear witness that we are Muslims.

قُلْ يَا أَهْلَ الْكِتَابِ تَعَالَوْا إِلَىٰ كَلِمَةٍ سَوَاءٍ بَيْنَنَا وَبَيْنَكُمْ أَلَّا نَعْبُدَ إِلَّا اللَّهَ وَلَا نُشْرِكَ بِهِ شَيْئًا وَلَا يَتَّخِذَ بَعْضُنَا بَعْضًا أَرْبَابًا مِّن دُونِ اللَّهِ ۚ فَإِن تَوَلَّوْا فَقُولُوا اشْهَدُوا بِأَنَّا مُسْلِمُونَ

Al-Imran 64

They are not all alike; of the followers of the Book there is an upright party; they recite Allah's communications in the night time and they adore (Him).

They believe in Allah and the last day, and they enjoin what is right and forbid the wrong, and they strive with one

لَيْسُوا سَوَاءً ۗ مِّنْ أَهْلِ الْكِتَابِ أُمَّةٌ قَائِمَةٌ يَتْلُونَ آيَاتِ اللَّهِ آنَاءَ اللَّيْلِ وَهُمْ يَسْجُدُونَ

يُؤْمِنُونَ بِاللَّهِ وَالْيَوْمِ الْآخِرِ وَيَأْمُرُونَ بِالْمَعْرُوفِ

(continued next page)

Chapter One

another in hastening to good deeds, and those are among the good.

And whatever good they do, they shall not be denied it, and Allah knows those who guard (against evil).

Al-Imran 113-115

And We said to the Israelites after him: Dwell in the land: and when the promise of the next life shall come to pass, we will bring you both together in judgment.

Al-Osara 104

Nothing is (incumbent) on the Apostle but to deliver (the message), and Allah knows what you do openly and what you hide.

Say: The bad and the good are not equal, though the abundance of the bad may please you; so be careful of (your duty to) Allah, O men of understanding, that you may be successful.

Al-Maidah 99-100

And every nation had an apostle; so when their apostle came, the matter was decided between them with justice and they shall not be dealt with unjustly.

Yunus 47

Surely they who divided their religion into parts and became sects, you have no concern with them; their affair is only with Allah, then He will inform them of what they did.

Whoever brings a good deed, he shall have ten like it, and whoever brings an evil deed, he shall be recompensed only with the like of it, and they shall not be dealt with unjustly.

Al-Anam 159-160

(As to) these, surely that about which they are shall be brought to naught and that which they do is vain.

He said: What! shall I seek for you a god other than Allah while He has made you excel (all) created things?

(continued next page)

And when We delivered you from Firon's people who subjected you to severe torment, killing your sons and sparing your women, and in this there was a great trial from your Lord.

And We appointed with Musa a time of thirty nights and completed them with ten (more), so the appointed time of his Lord was complete forty nights, and Musa said to his brother Haroun: Take my place among my people, and act well and do not follow the way of the mischief-makers.

Al-Araf 139-142

And ordain for us good in this world's life and in the hereafter, for surely we turn to Thee. He said: (As for) My chastisement, I will afflict with it whom I please, and My mercy encompasses all things; so I will ordain it (specially) for those who guard (against evil) and pay the poor-rate, and those who believe in Our communications.

Al-Araf 156

And of Musa's people was a party who guided (people) with the truth, and thereby did they do justice.

Al-Araf 159

And upon Allah it rests to show the right way, and there are some deviating (ways); and if He please He would certainly guide you all aright.

Al-Nahl 9

Surely Allah enjoins the doing of justice and the doing of good (to others) and the giving to the kindred, and He forbids indecency and evil and rebellion; He admonishes you that you may be mindful.

Al-Nahl 90

And if Allah please He would certainly make you a single nation, but He causes to err whom He pleases and guides whom He pleases; and most certainly you will be questioned as to what you did.

Al-Nahl 93

Chapter One

Except those who are patient and do good; they shall have forgiveness and a great reward.

Then, it may be that you will give up part of what is revealed to you and your breast will become straitened by it because they say: Why has not a treasure been sent down upon him or an angel come with him? You are only a warner; and Allah is custodian over all things.

Hud 11-12

Whoever goes aright, for his own soul does he go aright; and whoever goes astray, to its detriment only does he go astray; nor can the bearer of a burden bear the burden of another, nor do We chastise until We raise an apostle.

Al-Osara 15

Surely Allah does not forgive that anything should be associated with Him, and forgives what is besides that to whomsoever He pleases; and whoever associates anything with Allah, he devises indeed a great sin.

Have you not considered those who attribute purity to themselves? Nay, Allah purifies whom He pleases; and they shall not be wronged the husk of a date stone.

Al-Nisa 48-49

If you do good openly or do it in secret or pardon an evil, then surely Allah is Pardoning, Powerful.

Al-Nisa 149

And every nation had an apostle; so when their apostle came, the matter was decided between them with justice and they shall not be dealt with unjustly.

Yunus 25

And most surely we are a vigilant multitude.
So We turned them out of gardens and springs,
And treasures and goodly dwellings,

Al-Furqan 56-58

When the Prophet Mohammed took offense at the actions of some Jewish sinners and, as a result, some condemnatory verses were written, it could thus still be shown again that the religion of Islam respected Jewish belief as well as the nation of Israel. I should mention that all religions, and specially those that possess a heavenly book, are based on common values; consequently, minor differences in ideas and taste should not be considered as weakening any common basis of belief. In view of this, does it make sense that people quarrel and argue about trivial variations of faith – and thus, misuse religion – so that instead of bringing happiness to human beings it becomes an instrument of violence and spite? Is it ever appropriate to kill, torture and exploit in the name of religion?

Chapter Two

Freedom of Thought in Islam

In today's world, freedom to think one's own thoughts is fundamental; every broad-minded person should try to reach this aim. One of the ways of doing this is through negotiation and the exchanging of ideas. In this way different groups and sects demonstrate only a part of the truth, for none of God's children are able to see the whole truth if they adhere to only one point of view. In Islam, great emphasis has always been placed on freedom of thought. Indeed the Almighty God has forbidden the persecution, torture or killing of innocent people for having different ideas or for believing in other heavenly religions. The Islamic religion exhorts people to show good intentions.

Recommending the lawful and forbidding the sinful is necessary guidance for everyone. Thinking, inviting others to negotiate and trying to change their concepts are not crimes. It is in fact a duty. We should avoid quarrels, conflict and accusations of heresy. We should try for unity instead.

And do not dispute with the followers of the Book except by what is best, except those of them who act unjustly, and say: We believe in that which has been revealed to us and revealed to you, and our God and your God is One, and to Him do we submit.

وَلَا تُجَادِلُوٓا۟ أَهْلَ ٱلْكِتَٰبِ إِلَّا بِٱلَّتِى هِىَ أَحْسَنُ إِلَّا ٱلَّذِينَ ظَلَمُوا۟ مِنْهُمْ وَقُولُوٓا۟ ءَامَنَّا بِٱلَّذِىٓ أُنزِلَ إِلَيْنَا وَأُنزِلَ إِلَيْكُمْ وَإِلَٰهُنَا وَإِلَٰهُكُمْ وَٰحِدٌ وَنَحْنُ لَهُۥ مُسْلِمُونَ

Al-Ankabut 46

Islam is a religion of unity, based on monotheism. The uniqueness of God has spread a glow over the world and He has caused its unity. Because the Almighty God is unique, His unity rules the world – all of nature strives towards his special order. Despite differences of race, and physical and geographical variations in human beings, the *Gracious Koran* recognizes all as brothers and sisters with common parents; a principle emphasized by other heavenly religions.

(All) people are a single nation; so Allah raised prophets as bearers of good news and as warners, and He revealed with them the Book with truth, that it might judge between people in that in which they differed; and none but the very people who were given it differed about it after clear arguments had come to them, revolting

كَانَ ٱلنَّاسُ أُمَّةً وَٰحِدَةً فَبَعَثَ ٱللَّهُ ٱلنَّبِيِّـۧنَ مُبَشِّرِينَ وَمُنذِرِينَ وَأَنزَلَ مَعَهُمُ ٱلْكِتَٰبَ بِٱلْحَقِّ لِيَحْكُمَ بَيْنَ ٱلنَّاسِ فِيمَا ٱخْتَلَفُوا۟ فِيهِ وَمَا ٱخْتَلَفَ فِيهِ إِلَّا ٱلَّذِينَ أُوتُوهُ مِنۢ بَعْدِ مَا جَآءَتْهُمُ ٱلْبَيِّنَٰتُ

(continued next page)

among themselves; so Allah has guided by His will those who believe to the truth about which they differed; and Allah guides whom He pleases to the right path.

Al-Baqarah 213

The Almighty God says in *Al-Hurjurat 13*:

O you men! surely We have created you of a male and a female, and made you tribes and families that you may know each other; surely the most honorable of you with Allah is the one among you most careful (of his duty); surely Allah is Knowing, Aware.

Many verses of the *Gracious Koran* are addressed to all human beings.

And surely We have honored the children of Adam, and We carry them in the land and the sea, and We have given them of the good things, and We have made them to excel by an appropriate excellence over most of those whom We have created.

Al-Oscara 70

In the *Gracious Koran* all the followers of monotheistic religions are considered as equal, and are recommended to stress what is common to them all – to believe in a single God and unite in their rejection of atheism, blasphemy and polytheism. As we see in the *Sura Al-Imran 64*.

Say: O followers of the Book! come to an equitable proposition between us and you that we shall not serve any but Allah and (that) we shall not associate aught with Him, and (that) some of us shall not take others for lords besides Allah; but if they turn back, then say: Bear witness that we are Muslims.

Let us listen to and obey this pleasant injunction from the the *Sura Omran*:

The believers are but brethren, therefore make peace between your brethren and be careful of (your duty to) Allah that mercy may be had on you.

Here are clear instructions from the Almighty God to maintain friendship among the followers of the heavenly book and to always avoid altercation.

Chapter Three

Are Those Possessing a Heavenly Book Pure?

Reading and understanding the Holy verses help us determine the claim that Jews are impure as untrue, based on groundless accusation. Many sages have written about the purity of the people possessing a heavenly book, among them Chief Ayatollah Seyyed Mohsen Hakim, who has written a thesis about this question based on his comprehensive research.

1- All sages of Islam confirm that the Children of Israel possess a heavenly book and are monotheists .
2- In *Sura Al-Sajdah 6-10*, we read:

> These are the communications of Allah which We recite to you with truth; then in what announcement would they believe after Allah and His communications?
> Woe to every sinful liar,
> Who hears the communications of Allah recited to him, then persists proudly as though he had not heard them; so announce to him a painful punishment.
> And when he comes to know of any of Our communications, he takes it for a jest; these it is that shall have abasing chastisement.
> Before them is hell, and there shall not avail them aught of what they earned, nor those whom they took for guardians besides Allah, and they shall have a grievous punishment.

These verses prove it is against the dignity of God to consider his followers and those who carry a pure soul and will return to him after death, impure. We know that the Almighty God is far removed from any kind of impurity.

In the *Sura Al-Maidah 5*, we can find another strong proof :

> This day (all) the good things are allowed to you; and the food of those who have been given the Book is lawful for you and your food is lawful for them; and the chaste from among the believing women and the chaste from among those who have been given the Book before you (are lawful for you); when you have given them their

(continued next page)

Are Those Possessing a Heavenly Book Pure?

dowries, taking (them) in marriage, not fornicating nor taking them for paramours in secret; and whoever denies faith, his work indeed is of no account, and in the hereafter he shall be one of the losers.

This verse is very clear that those possessing a heavenly book are not impure. According to the verse, a Jewish or Christian woman may keep her own faith while living in the house of her Moslem husband, since she is also from a people who possess a heavenly book. We read in *Sura Al-Ahqaf 12-16* as follows:

And before it the Book of Musa was a guide and a mercy: and this is a Book verifying (it) in the Arabic language that it may warn those who are unjust and as good news for the doers of good.

Surely those who say, Our Lord is Allah, then they continue on the right way, they shall have no fear nor shall they grieve.

These are the dwellers of the garden, abiding therein: a reward for what they did.

And We have enjoined on man doing of good to his parents; with trouble did his mother bear him and with trouble did she bring him forth; and the bearing of him and the weaning of him was thirty months; until when he attains his maturity and reaches forty years, he says: My Lord! grant me that I may give thanks for Thy favor which Thou hast bestowed on me and on my parents, and that I may do good which pleases Thee and do good to me in respect of my offspring; surely I turn to Thee, and surely I am of those who submit.

These are they from whom We accept the best of what they have done and pass over their evil deeds, among the dwellers of the garden; the promise of truth which they were promised.

In *Sura Al-Taubah 27-29* Almighty God announces:

Then will Allah after this turn (mercifully) to whom He pleases, and Allah is Forgiving, Merciful.

CHAPTER THREE

> O you who believe! the idolaters are nothing but unclean, so they shall not approach the Sacred Mosque after this year; and if you fear poverty then Allah will enrich you out of His grace if He please; surely Allah is Knowing, Wise.

> Fight those who do not believe in Allah, nor in the latter day, nor do they prohibit what Allah and His Apostle have prohibited, nor follow the religion of truth, out of those who have been given the Book, until they pay the tax in acknowledgment of superiority and they are in a state of subjection.

As I have mentioned before, such verses were directed at idolaters – not to people possessing a heavenly book. In fact, monotheists did not go to the House of God (Kaaba) to worship idols.

In *Sura Al-Dukhan 30-32* God speaks of the blessings which he gave to the Children of Israel.

> Then as to those who believed and did good, their Lord will make them enter into His mercy; that is the manifest achievement.

> As to those who disbelieved: What! were not My communications recited to you? But you were proud and you were a guilty people.

> And when it was said, Surely the promise of Allah is true and as for the hour, there is no doubt about it, you said: We do not know what the hour is; we do not think (that it will come to pass) save a passing thought, and we are not at all sure.

In *Sura Al-Maidah 18* there is another sign of God's blessings to the Children of Israel.

> And the Jews and the Christians say: We are the sons of Allah and his beloved ones. Say: Why does He then chastise you for your faults? Nay, you are mortals from among those whom He has created; He forgives whom He pleases and chastises whom He pleases; and Allah's is the kingdom of the heavens and the earth and what is between them, and to Him is the eventual coming.

We can clearly understand from the following verses in *Sura Al-Maidah 69* that those possessing a heavenly book believe in God and also in the Day of

Are Those Possessing a Heavenly Book Pure?

Resurrection which will save them if they do charitable deeds. There is no reason for them to worry or be sad.

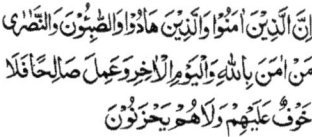

Surely those who believe and those who are Jews and the Sebeans and the Christians whoever believes in Allah and the last day and does good—they shall have no fear nor shall they grieve.

Regarding the verses of the *Holy Koran,* considering what was mentioned here previously, devout people possessing a heavenly book, who believe in God, his prophets and the Day of Resurrection, are pure. Such people may have peaceful friendships with Moslems. Some people have mentioned that those who do not believe in Mohammed as a prophet are impure. Fortunately today, due to the improvement of communication and the dissemination of the media, everybody should know that Mohammed is the prophet of the world of Islam. 1.5 billion followers believe in his mission and His Book.

Chapter Four

The Kind Attention of the Almighty God to the Children of Israel in the *Gracious Koran*

Let us look at the roots of difference. Owing to the merciful contents of the verses of the *Gracious Koran*, from the time of the Prophet Mohammed and the Rashedin caliphs including the period of the Omavian and Abassid Caliphates, religious minorities lived peaceful lives in Islamic countries until the 12th or 13th century. The believers of the heavenly religions to some extent enjoyed a calm and peaceful co-existence with the Moslems. With the spreading of Moslems over ever-larger areas and the increase in religious prejudice, on the part of various governments, the relationship became strained. The situation was, at this time, aggravated by the Crusades. It is probable that there were other contributing factors, but it can be said that these disputes, arguments and misunderstandings began during the reign of Fatemi and came to a head against the Children of Israel.

The Verses of the *Gracious Koran*

In order to show the attitude of the *Gracious Koran* towards the Children of Israel we have to refer to both encouraging and reproaching Verses. Here are some verses from the *Suras Al-Baqarah, Al-Araf, Al-Maidah, Al-Osara, Al Al-Al-Imran, Al-Ankabut, Al-Jathiyah, Al-Anbiya* and *Yunus*:
On the steadfastness of the prophet Moses and the Children of Israel, and their receiving God's blessings, *Sura Al-Araf 7*: speaks to us.

| Then most certainly We will relate to them with knowledge, and We were not absent. |  |

On being reminded of the granting of the blessings of God to the Children of Israel we read:

| But when good befell them they said: This is due to us; and when evil afflicted them, they attributed it to the ill-luck of Musa and those with him; surely their evil fortune is only from Allah, but most of them do not know. | 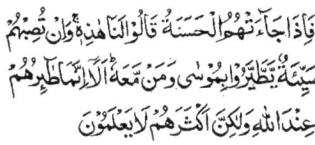 |

Al-Araf 131

THE KIND ATTENTION OF THE ALMIGHTY GOD...

And they said: Whatever sign you may bring to us to charm us with it—we will not believe in you.

Al-Araf 132

Therefore We sent upon them widespread death, and the locusts and the lice and the frog and the blood, clear signs; but they behaved haughtily and they were a guilty people.

Al-Araf 133

And when the plague fell upon them, they said: O Musa! pray for us to your Lord as He has promised with you, if you remove the plague from us, we will certainly believe in you and we will certainly send away with you the children of Israel.

Al-Araf 134

But when We removed the plague from them till a term which they should attain, lo! they broke (the promise).

Al-Araf 135

Therefore We inflicted retribution on them and drowned them in the sea because they rejected Our signs and were heedless of them.

Al-Araf 136

And We made the people who were deemed weak to inherit the eastern lands and the western ones which We had blessed; and the good word of your Lord was fulfilled in the children of Israel because they bore up (sufferings) patiently; and We utterly destroyed what Firon and his people had wrought and what they

Al-Araf 137

And ordain for us good in this world's life and in the hereafter, for surely we turn to Thee. He said: (As for) My chastisement, I will afflict with it whom I please, and My mercy encompasses all things; so I will ordain it (specially) for those who guard (against evil) and pay the poor-rate, and those who believe in Our communications.

Al-Araf 156

Twenty-six

CHAPTER FOUR

Say: O people! surely I am the Apostle of Allah to you all, of Him Whose is the kingdom of the heavens and the earth, there is no god but He; He brings to life and causes to die, therefore believe in Allah and His apostle, the Ummi Prophet who believes in Allah and His words, and follow him so that you may walk in the right way.

قُلْ يَا أَيُّهَا النَّاسُ إِنِّي رَسُولُ اللَّهِ إِلَيْكُمْ جَمِيعًا الَّذِي لَهُ مُلْكُ السَّمَاوَاتِ وَالْأَرْضِ لَا إِلَٰهَ إِلَّا هُوَ يُحْيِي وَيُمِيتُ فَآمِنُوا بِاللَّهِ وَرَسُولِهِ النَّبِيِّ الْأُمِّيِّ الَّذِي يُؤْمِنُ بِاللَّهِ وَكَلِمَاتِهِ وَاتَّبِعُوهُ لَعَلَّكُمْ تَهْتَدُونَ

Al-Araf 158

And of Musa's people was a party who guided (people) with the truth, and thereby did they do justice.

وَمِنْ قَوْمِ مُوسَىٰ أُمَّةٌ يَهْدُونَ بِالْحَقِّ وَبِهِ يَعْدِلُونَ

Al-Araf 159

And We divided them into twelve tribes, as nations; and We revealed to Musa when his people asked him for water: Strike the rock with your staff, so outflowed from it twelve springs; each tribe knew its drinking place; and We made the clouds to give shade over them and We sent to them manna and quails: Eat of the good things We have given you. And they did not do Us any harm, but they did injustice to their own souls.

وَقَطَّعْنَاهُمُ اثْنَتَيْ عَشْرَةَ أَسْبَاطًا أُمَمًا وَأَوْحَيْنَا إِلَىٰ مُوسَىٰ إِذِ اسْتَسْقَاهُ قَوْمُهُ أَنِ اضْرِبْ بِعَصَاكَ الْحَجَرَ فَانْبَجَسَتْ مِنْهُ اثْنَتَا عَشْرَةَ عَيْنًا قَدْ عَلِمَ كُلُّ أُنَاسٍ مَشْرَبَهُمْ وَظَلَّلْنَا عَلَيْهِمُ الْغَمَامَ وَأَنْزَلْنَا عَلَيْهِمُ الْمَنَّ وَالسَّلْوَىٰ كُلُوا مِنْ طَيِّبَاتِ مَا رَزَقْنَاكُمْ وَمَا ظَلَمُونَا وَلَٰكِنْ كَانُوا أَنْفُسَهُمْ يَظْلِمُونَ

Al-Araf 160

And when it was said to them: Reside in this town and eat from it wherever you wish, and say: Put down from us our heavy burdens; and enter the gate making obeisance, We will forgive you your wrongs: We will give more to those who do good (to others).

وَإِذْ قِيلَ لَهُمُ اسْكُنُوا هَٰذِهِ الْقَرْيَةَ وَكُلُوا مِنْهَا حَيْثُ شِئْتُمْ وَقُولُوا حِطَّةٌ وَادْخُلُوا الْبَابَ سُجَّدًا نَغْفِرْ لَكُمْ خَطِيئَاتِكُمْ سَنَزِيدُ الْمُحْسِنِينَ

Al-Araf 161

But those who were unjust among them changed it for a saying other than that which had been spoken to them; so We sent upon them a pestilence from heaven because they were unjust.

فَبَدَّلَ الَّذِينَ ظَلَمُوا مِنْهُمْ قَوْلًا غَيْرَ الَّذِي قِيلَ لَهُمْ فَأَرْسَلْنَا عَلَيْهِمْ رِجْزًا مِنَ السَّمَاءِ بِمَا كَانُوا يَظْلِمُونَ

Al-Araf 162

And ask them about the town which stood by the sea; when they exceeded the limits of the Sabbath, when their fish came to them on the day of their Sabbath,

وَاسْأَلْهُمْ عَنِ الْقَرْيَةِ الَّتِي كَانَتْ حَاضِرَةَ الْبَحْرِ إِذْ يَعْدُونَ فِي السَّبْتِ إِذْ تَأْتِيهِمْ

(continued next page)

THE KIND ATTENTION OF THE ALMIGHTY GOD...

appearing on the surface of the water, and on the day on which they did not keep the Sabbath they did not come to them; thus did We try them because they transgressed.

Al-Araf 163

And (as to) those who disbelieve in and reject My communications, they are the inmates of the fire, in it they shall abide.

Al-Baqarah 39

O children of Israel! call to mind My favor which I bestowed on you and be faithful to (your) covenant with Me, I will fulfill (My) covenant with you; and of Me, Me alone, should you be afraid.

Al-Baqarah 40

And believe in what I have revealed, verifying that which is with you, and be not the first to deny it, neither take a mean price in exchange for My communications; and Me, Me alone should you fear.

Al-Baqarah 41

And do not mix up the truth with the falsehood, nor hide the truth while you know (it).

Al-Baqarah 42

And keep up prayer and pay the poor-rate and bow down with those who bow down.

Al-Baqarah 43

What! do you enjoin men to be good and neglect your own souls while you read the Book; have you then no sense?

Al-Baqarah 44

And seek assistance through patience and prayer, and most surely it is a hard thing except for the humble ones,

Al-Baqarah 45

CHAPTER FOUR

Who know that they shall meet their Lord and that they shall return to Him.

Al-Baqarah 46

O children of Israel! call to mind My favor which I bestowed on you and that I made you excel the nations.

Al-Baqarah 47

And be on your guard against a day when one soul shall not avail another in the least, neither shall intercession on its behalf be accepted, nor shall any compensation be taken from it, nor shall they be helped.

Al-Baqarah 48

Surely those who believe, and those who are Jews, and the Christians, and the Sabians, whoever believes in Allah and the Last day and does good, they shall have their reward from their Lord, and there is no fear for them, nor shall they grieve.

Al-Baqarah 62

And when We said: Enter this city, then eat from it a plenteous (food) wherever you wish, and enter the gate making obeisance, and say, forgiveness. We will forgive you your wrongs and give more to those who do good (to others).

Al-Baqarah 58

Those to whom We have given the Book read it as it ought to be read. These believe in it; and whoever disbelieves in it, these it is that are the losers.

Al-Baqarah 121

God again reminds us that he has conferred his blessings on the Children of Israel by granting them a culture of brilliance.

And when his Lord tried Ibrahim with certain words, he fulfilled them. He

(continued next page)

> said: Surely I will make you an Imam of men. Ibrahim said: And of my offspring? My covenant does not include the unjust, said He.

Al-Baqarah 124

Now to the acceptance of obligations by the Jews and the appointment of twelve leaders: The Almighty God clearly has cast the Children of Israel in the role of the nation of authority.

> And certainly Allah made a covenant with the children of Israel, and We raised up among them twelve chieftains; and Allah said: Surely I am with you; if you keep up prayer and pay the poor-rate and believe in My apostles and assist them and offer to Allah a goodly gift, I will most certainly cover your evil deeds, and I will most certainly cause you to enter into gardens beneath which rivers flow, but whoever disbelieves from among you after that, he indeed shall lose the right way.

Al-Maidah 12

> And when Musa said to his people: O my people! remember the favor of Allah upon you when He raised prophets among you and made you kings and gave you what He had not given to any other among the nations.

Al-Maidah 20

In this verse God recalls the blessings He conferred on the Children of Israel, and remarks that prophets, kings and rulers have appeared among them. The highest number of prophets and kings was to be found among the Children of Israel. The granting of knowledge, power and glory to the Children of Israel are tokens of Divine wishes – as mentioned in *Sura Al-Anbiya 21*.

> Or have they taken gods from the earth who raise (the dead).

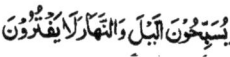

Sura Al-Jathiyah tells of the granting of power to the Children of Israel:

> Allah is He Who made subservient to you the sea that the ships may run therein by His command, and that you may seek of His grace, and that you may give thanks.

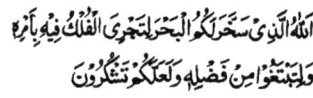

Al-Jathiyah 12

And He has made subservient to you whatsoever is in the heavens and whatsoever is in the earth, all, from Himself; most surely there are signs in this for a people who reflect.

وَسَخَّرَ لَكُم مَّا فِى ٱلسَّمَٰوَٰتِ وَمَا فِى ٱلْأَرْضِ جَمِيعًا مِّنْهُ إِنَّ فِى ذَٰلِكَ لَآيَٰتٍ لِّقَوْمٍ يَتَفَكَّرُونَ

Al-Jathiyah 13

Say to those who believe (that) they forgive those who do not fear the days of Allah that He may reward a people for what they earn.

قُل لِّلَّذِينَ ءَامَنُوا۟ يَغْفِرُوا۟ لِلَّذِينَ لَا يَرْجُونَ أَيَّامَ ٱللَّهِ لِيَجْزِىَ قَوْمًۢا بِمَا كَانُوا۟ يَكْسِبُونَ

Al-Jathiyah 14

Whoever does good, it is for his own soul, and whoever does evil, it is against himself; then you shall be brought back to your Lord.

مَنْ عَمِلَ صَٰلِحًا فَلِنَفْسِهِۦ وَمَنْ أَسَآءَ فَعَلَيْهَا ثُمَّ إِلَىٰ رَبِّكُمْ تُرْجَعُونَ

Al-Jathiya 15

Relationship with the Followers of a Heavenly Book

And certainly We gave the Book and the wisdom and the prophecy to the children of Israel, and We gave them of the goodly things, and We made them excel the nations.

وَلَقَدْ ءَاتَيْنَا بَنِىٓ إِسْرَٰٓءِيلَ ٱلْكِتَٰبَ وَٱلْحُكْمَ وَٱلنُّبُوَّةَ وَرَزَقْنَٰهُم مِّنَ ٱلطَّيِّبَٰتِ وَفَضَّلْنَٰهُمْ عَلَى ٱلْعَٰلَمِينَ

Al-Jathiyah 16

In *Sura Al-Ankabut 46* we read:

And do not dispute with the followers of the Book except by what is best, except those of them who act unjustly, and say: We believe in that which has been revealed to us and revealed to you, and our God and your God is One, and to Him do we submit.

وَلَا تُجَٰدِلُوٓا۟ أَهْلَ ٱلْكِتَٰبِ إِلَّا بِٱلَّتِى هِىَ أَحْسَنُ إِلَّا ٱلَّذِينَ ظَلَمُوا۟ مِنْهُمْ وَقُولُوٓا۟ ءَامَنَّا بِٱلَّذِىٓ أُنزِلَ إِلَيْنَا وَأُنزِلَ إِلَيْكُمْ وَإِلَٰهُنَا وَإِلَٰهُكُمْ وَٰحِدٌ وَنَحْنُ لَهُۥ مُسْلِمُونَ

When looking at the verses previously cited about rewards and the gifts of the Almighty God to the Children of Israel, there emerges clearly His will to save the nation of Israel from deviation, misfortune and difficulties; this is particularly true regarding the problems experienced at the time of the Pharaohs. The verses also demonstrate the divine will of granting the people of Israel power and authority.

Moses was a powerful prophet who did all he could to achieve the deliverance of the Children of Israel and enhance their glory. The story of how Moses' life was saved, how lives of the Children of Israel were saved, the difficulties the Pharaoh experienced which caused him to suffer great wretchedness and ultimately to be drowned together with his soldiers, is told beautifully in the *Holy Koran*.

I mention these signs and portents of the Almighty God to emphasize the fact that He has been kind to the Children of Israel, and has favoured them by transmuting them from an unknown tribe to a civilized and powerful nation with many prophets and rulers. But it must also be mentioned that during the course of history, Almighty God has granted such advantages and privileges to every nation, sect and group.

Chapter Five

•

Observing the *Holy Koran*: A Warning to the Unbelievers

Who is an Atheist?

We have seen that there are some verses in different *Suras* in the *Holy Koran* that can be regarded as sources of hope, as well as of fear and dread. There are verses in which sinners and atheists are reproached and are called upon to be aware of the consequences of their ill-advised deeds – deeds that lead to severe punishment in the next world. Many verses in the Holy Book emphasize the command to worship the sole God and exhort the reader to believe in his prophets and his angels, and also in the coming of the Last Day.

Reading and studying these verses teaches us that a person who worships the sole God, believes in God's divine prophets and angels, and in the coming of the Last Day, not only is not an atheist, but will be saved in the other world. Thus, an atheist is a person who does not worship the sole God, does not believe in His prophets and angels, nor in the coming of the Last Day. Such a person must expect to be punished by means of the fires of Hell.

And whoever does not believe in Allah and His Apostle, then surely We have prepared burning fire for the unbelievers.

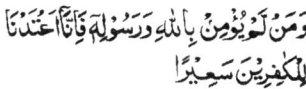

Al Fateh 13

In the *Gracious Koran* those who are two-faced and deceitful – who are called Hypocrites – are also considered as being atheists.

What is the matter with you, then, that you have become two parties about the hypocrites, while Allah has made them return (to unbelief) for what they have earned? Do you wish to guide him whom Allah has caused to err? And whomsoever Allah causes to err, you shall by no means find a way for him.

They desire that you should disbelieve as they have disbelieved, so that you might be (all) alike; therefore take not from among them friends until they fly (their homes) in Allah's way; but if they turn back, then seize them and kill them wherever you find them, and take not from among them a friend or a helper.

Al-Nisa 88-89

Different opinions are held as to why these verses were promulgated. There are those who agree with Abolfath Razi, who believed they were intended to rebuke those deceitful disciples of the Prophet who left him at the time of the Ohod War, and in fact avoided accompanying him supportively in the war. They caused the followers of the Prophet Mohammed to be split into two groups.

Others, such as Abou Jafar and Fra, opined that the verses were sent because of those people who came from Mecca to live in Medina asserting that they were believers in Islam, but later did not like to live there and ultimately returned to Mecca under the pretext of going for a walk in the desert (The *Gracious Koran*, translated and interpreted by Baha Eddin Khorramshahi, page 92). In *Sura Ahzab* Almighty God regards two-faced people as mentally ill, to be removed from the divine presence. The *Sura Al-Aubah*, which contains one hundred and twenty-nine verses, enlarges upon the evil deeds of the Hypocrites (*Munafiqun*) and the sufferings the Prophet Mohammed underwent because of them. And yet it is interesting to note that out of those verses, only two (29 and 30) refer to the double-faced people who possess a heavenly book, and to the fact that God causes the Prophet Mohammed to become aware of their deeds.

There were tribes that, contrary to the religion of the Children of Israel, which is monotheistic, knew 'Ozair' as the Son of God. These people were wiped off the face of the earth because of their wrong belief. There were also tribes that represented themselves as being the possessors of a heavenly book, while in fact they were atheists. They did not believe in one God and his prophets, and they failed to obey either the orders of their own prophets, or the prescriptions contained in the *Bible* or *Holy Torah*. These people have vanished from the world completely. Today there is no one among the Children of Israel who believes that 'Ozair' is the Son of God or who would deny the uniqueness of the Almighty God, as proclaimed in the books of the *Holy Torah*.

Regrettably, *Sura Al-Taubah 29* has served various cruel rulers who interpreted it incorrectly as justification for tyrannizing the believers of religions with a heavenly book. However, this matter applied to the 'Munafiq' and not to the atheists. Today not a single 'Munafiq' is living in the world.

Reflections on Almighty God's Justice in the Verses of the *Gracious Koran*

A considerable part of the verses in the *Gracious Koran* is concerned with the justice of the Almighty God, and contains instructions for Moslems as to how to behave towards their fellows. Heavenly verses so attractive and brilliant, it is easy to understand why the *Koran* is considered a miracle. The verses are effective and persuasive as to soften even the hearts of the cruel. They contain a remark about God's justice, and Moslems are called upon to behave justly towards the followers of religions which possess a heavenly book.

CHAPTER FIVE

Using the Best Approach in Dealing with the Possessors of a Heavenly Book

The *Gracious Koran* has laid heavy emphasis on the need to use a wise approach and to demonstrate kindness towards the possessors of a heavenly book.

> And do not dispute with the followers of the Book except by what is best, except those of them who act unjustly, and say: We believe in that which has been revealed to us and revealed to you, and our God and your God is One, and to Him do we submit.

Al-Ankabut 46

The Approval of the People who Possess a Heavenly Book

Besides forbidding polytheism, Almighty God has emphasized the instruction to be kind to parents, and take care of orphans. The *Gracious Koran* orders its readers to abstain from evil deeds and murder.

> Say: Come I will recite what your Lord has forbidden to you—(remember) that you do not associate anything with Him and show kindness to your parents, and do not slay your children for (fear of) poverty—We provide for you and for them—and do not draw nigh to indecencies, those of them which are apparent and those which are concealed, and do not kill the soul which Allah has forbidden except for the requirements of justice; this He has enjoined you with that you may understand.
>
> And do not approach the property of the orphan except in the best manner until he attains his maturity; and give full measure and weight with justice—We do not impose on any soul a duty except to the extent of its ability; and when you speak, then be just though it be (against) a relative, and fulfill Allah's covenant; this He has enjoined you with that you may be mindful;

Al-Anam 151-152

Acting Justly When Dealing Even with Enemies

In *Sura Al-Maidah 8* Moslems are instructed to take justice into account when dealing with their enemies.

O you who believe! Be upright for Allah, bearers of witness with justice, and let not hatred of a people incite you not to act equitably; act equitably, that is nearer to piety, and be careful of (your duty to) Allah; surely Allah is Aware of what you do.

On Not Being Disappointed by Sinners

Great patience must be exercised in the matter of education and guidance. Speech and persuasion are very effective; for this reason the *Gracious Koran* does not lose hope when the correction of sinners is concerned, and assures them that they will all benefit from divine mercy.

Say: O my servants! who have acted extravagantly against their own souls, do not despair of the mercy of Allah; surely Allah forgives the faults altogether; surely He is the Forgiving, the Merciful.

And return to your Lord time after time and submit to Him before there comes to you the punishment, then you shall not be helped.

Al-Zumar 53-54

Chapter Six

•

Has the *Torah* been Altered?

Unfortunately, as was the case fourteen hundred years ago, many people today are easily influenced by their ignorance of the subject of the heavenly religions and their heavenly books. Lack of knowledge leads to incorrect interpretations. This phenomenon was true at the time of the Prophet Mohammed some 1,400 years ago, when he was negotiating with some illiterate, common Jews. Mohammed found out that their behaviour partly contrasted with the instructions of the *Holy Torah*.

As we mentioned earlier, at the time of the Prophet Mohammed negotiations among peoples were conducted orally, so that it is possible that due to this fact alterations were made. In the holy verses of the *Gracious Koran* there is no indication that the *Torah* has been altered. The text and contents of the *Holy Torah* have remained as it was initially; and the verses of the *Holy Koran* constitute good proof of this fact. Above all, the observations made at the time of the Prophet Mohammed about the Children of Israel was relevant to the Jews who then lived in Medina and its suburbs, while the nation of Israel, although not consisting of vast numbers, was scattered all over the world and performed their religious duties punctiliously.

The following explanation demonstrates that altering the *Torah* has not been possible in the past, and will not be possible in the future. The *Holy Torah* has been divided up according to the weeks of the year in such a way that every Sabbath a particular section (called a 'Parsha') is read. Therefore, any change or alteration of a word, or even of a letter, is impossible. Moreover, it is absolutely forbidden to read from a scroll of the *Torah* in which a word is illegible or has disappeared. If such a thing is verified, the *Torah* scroll is invalid and must be corrected or discarded.

While a particular section of the *Torah* is being recited, two persons usually stand beside the reader in order to watch that he reads every word and letter correctly. The other worshippers present must be quiet and listen carefully to the reader. Thus, any mistake, even in pronunciation, is unacceptable.

The weekly *Torah* readings described above are performed in an identical manner all over the world.

And when Isa son of Marium said: O children of Israel! surely I am the apostle of Allah to you, verifying that which is before me of the Tavrat and giving the good news	وَإِذْ قَالَ عِيسَى ابْنُ مَرْيَمَ يَبَنِىٓ إِسْرَآءِيلَ إِنِّى رَسُولُ ٱللَّهِ إِلَيْكُم مُّصَدِّقًا لِّمَا بَيْنَ يَدَىَّ مِنَ

(continued next page)

of an Apostle who will come after me, his name being Ahmad; but when he came to them with clear arguments they said: This is clear magic.

التَّوْرَىٰةِ وَمُبَشِّرًۢا بِرَسُولٍ يَأْتِى مِنۢ بَعْدِى اسْمُهُۥٓ أَحْمَدُ ۖ فَلَمَّا جَآءَهُم بِٱلْبَيِّنَٰتِ قَالُوا۟ هَٰذَا سِحْرٌ مُّبِينٌ

Al-Saff 6

Confirmation of the *Torah*

And We gave Musa the Book and made it a guidance to the children of Israel, saying: Do not take a protector besides Me;

وَءَاتَيْنَا مُوسَى ٱلْكِتَٰبَ وَجَعَلْنَٰهُ هُدًى لِّبَنِىٓ إِسْرَٰٓءِيلَ أَلَّا تَتَّخِذُوا۟ مِن دُونِى وَكِيلًا

Al-Osara 2

Surely We revealed the Tavrat in which was guidance and light; with it the prophets who submitted themselves (to Allah) judged (matters) for those who were Jews, and the masters of Divine knowledge and the doctors, because they were required to guard (part) of the Book of Allah, and they were witnesses thereof; therefore fear not the people and fear Me, and do not take a small price for My communications; and whoever did not judge by what Allah revealed, those are they that are the unbelievers.

إِنَّآ أَنزَلْنَا ٱلتَّوْرَىٰةَ فِيهَا هُدًى وَنُورٌ ۚ يَحْكُمُ بِهَا ٱلنَّبِيُّونَ ٱلَّذِينَ أَسْلَمُوا۟ لِلَّذِينَ هَادُوا۟ وَٱلرَّبَّٰنِيُّونَ وَٱلْأَحْبَارُ بِمَا ٱسْتُحْفِظُوا۟ مِن كِتَٰبِ ٱللَّهِ وَكَانُوا۟ عَلَيْهِ شُهَدَآءَ ۚ فَلَا تَخْشَوُا۟ ٱلنَّاسَ وَٱخْشَوْنِ وَلَا تَشْتَرُوا۟ بِـَٔايَٰتِى ثَمَنًا قَلِيلًا ۚ وَمَن لَّمْ يَحْكُم بِمَآ أَنزَلَ ٱللَّهُ فَأُو۟لَٰٓئِكَ هُمُ ٱلْكَٰفِرُونَ

Al-Maidah 44

And We sent after them in their footsteps Isa, son of Marium, verifying what was before him of the Tavrat and We gave him the Injeel in which was guidance and light, and verifying what was before it of Tavrat and a guidance and an admonition for those who guard (against evil).

وَقَفَّيْنَا عَلَىٰٓ ءَاثَٰرِهِم بِعِيسَى ٱبْنِ مَرْيَمَ مُصَدِّقًا لِّمَا بَيْنَ يَدَيْهِ مِنَ ٱلتَّوْرَىٰةِ ۖ وَءَاتَيْنَٰهُ ٱلْإِنجِيلَ فِيهِ هُدًى وَنُورٌ وَمُصَدِّقًا لِّمَا بَيْنَ يَدَيْهِ مِنَ ٱلتَّوْرَىٰةِ وَهُدًى وَمَوْعِظَةً لِّلْمُتَّقِينَ

Al-Maidah 46

O Apostle! deliver what has been revealed to you from your Lord; and if you do it not, then you have not delivered His message, and Allah will protect you from the people; surely Allah will not guide the unbelieving people.

يَٰٓأَيُّهَا ٱلرَّسُولُ بَلِّغْ مَآ أُنزِلَ إِلَيْكَ مِن رَّبِّكَ ۖ وَإِن لَّمْ تَفْعَلْ فَمَا بَلَّغْتَ رِسَالَتَهُۥ ۚ وَٱللَّهُ يَعْصِمُكَ مِنَ ٱلنَّاسِ ۗ إِنَّ ٱللَّهَ لَا يَهْدِى ٱلْقَوْمَ ٱلْكَٰفِرِينَ

Al-Maidah 67

Say: We believe in Allah and (in) that which had been revealed to us, and (in)

قُولُوٓا۟ ءَامَنَّا بِٱللَّهِ وَمَآ أُنزِلَ إِلَيْنَا وَمَآ أُنزِلَ إِلَىٰٓ إِبْرَٰهِۦمَ

(continued next page)

that which was revealed to Ibrahim and Ismail and Ishaq and Yaqoub and the tribes, and (in) that which was given to Musa and Isa, and (in) that which was given to the prophets from their Lord, we do not make any distinction between any of them, and to Him do we submit.

Al-Baqarah 136

Those to whom We have given the Book read it as it ought to be read. These believe in it; and whoever disbelieves in it, these it is that are the losers.

O children of Israel, call to mind My favor which I bestowed on you and that I made you excel the nations.

Al-Baqarah 121-122

And how do they make you a judge and they have the Tavrat wherein is Allah's judgment? Yet they turn back after that, and these are not the believers.

Al-Maidah 4

To this then go on inviting, and go on steadfastly on the right way as you are commanded, and do not follow their low desires, and say: I believe in what Allah has revealed of the Book, and I am commanded to do justice between you: Allah is our Lord and your Lord; we shall have our deeds and you shall have your deeds; no plea need there be (now) between us and you: Allah will gather us together, and to Him is the return.

Al-Shura 15

Surely those who believe and those who are Jews and the Sebeans and the Christians whoever believes in Allah and the last day and does good—they shall have no fear nor shall they grieve.

Al-Maidah 69

Forbidden to you is that which dies of itself, and blood, and flesh of swine, and that on which any other name than that of Allah has been invoked, and the strangled (animal) and that beaten to death, and that

(continued next page)

| killed by a fall and that killed by being smitten with the horn, and that which wild beasts have eaten, except what you slaughter, and what is sacrificed on stones set up (for idols) and that you divide by the arrows; that is a transgression. This day have those who disbelieve despaired of your religion, so fear them not, and fear Me. This day have I perfected for you your religion and completed My favor on you and chosen for you Islam as a religion; but whoever is compelled by hunger, not inclining willfully to sin, then surely Allah is Forgiving, Merciful. | الْمُتَرَدِّيَةُ وَالنَّطِيحَةُ وَمَا أَكَلَ السَّبُعُ إِلَّا مَا ذَكَّيْتُمْ وَمَا ذُبِحَ عَلَى النُّصُبِ وَأَنْ تَسْتَقْسِمُوا بِالْأَزْلَامِ ذَلِكُمْ فِسْقٌ الْيَوْمَ يَئِسَ الَّذِينَ كَفَرُوا مِنْ دِينِكُمْ فَلَا تَخْشَوْهُمْ وَاخْشَوْنِ الْيَوْمَ أَكْمَلْتُ لَكُمْ دِينَكُمْ وَأَتْمَمْتُ عَلَيْكُمْ نِعْمَتِي وَرَضِيتُ لَكُمُ الْإِسْلَامَ دِينًا فَمَنِ اضْطُرَّ فِي مَخْمَصَةٍ غَيْرَ مُتَجَانِفٍ لِإِثْمٍ فَإِنَّ اللَّهَ غَفُورٌ رَحِيمٌ |

Al-Maidah 3

The name of Ahmed – the Prophet Mohammed – has been mentioned in the Holy Books of the gospel, but in those Holy Books there are some mysteries that are hidden now but will be revealed in the future. This matter is not particularly important, and no proof is required regarding the high and holy status of the Prophet Mohammed and the high position of the *Gracious Koran*. In fact, the proof is inside the problem. More than one quarter of the world's population are Moslems. That in itself is proof that the Islamic religion is true, and it attests to the rightful mission of the Prophet Mohammed.

While the believers believe that God predetermines the fate of human beings, the great expansion of Islam in the world is proof of the truth of the Islamic religion and of its Prophet Mohammed, and also represents a substantiation of the fact that the *Gracious Koran* is a miracle.

Proofs for the Truth of the *Holy Torah*

The Prophet Jesus says in the first chapter of the Gospel of Matthew, 17-18:

Think not that I am come to destroy the law, or the prophets; I am not come to destroy, but to fulfill. For verily I say unto you, till heaven and earth pass, one jot or one title shall in no wise pass from the law, till all be fulfilled.

There are some verses in the *Gracious Koran* that prove that the Holy *Torah* has not been altered. In the *Sura Al-Ahqaf 12* of the *Holy Koran* we read:

| And before it the Book of Musa was a guide and a mercy: and this is a Book verifying (it) in the Arabic language that it may warn those who are unjust and as good news for the doers of good. | وَمِنْ قَبْلِهِ كِتَابُ مُوسَى إِمَامًا وَرَحْمَةً وَهَذَا كِتَابٌ مُصَدِّقٌ لِسَانًا عَرَبِيًّا لِيُنْذِرَ الَّذِينَ ظَلَمُوا وَبُشْرَى لِلْمُحْسِنِينَ |

CHAPTER SIX

Thus we see that the *Gracious Koran* clearly confirms and respects the truth of the *Holy Torah*.

The Children of Israel believe that the Prophet Moses received the Ten Commandments from the Almighty God, and that he wrote the remainder of the *Torah* during the following forty years. The original *Torah* was delivered in thirteen copies – one copy was placed in the Mishkan [the box for the Ten Commandments], and the other twelve copies were handed to the leaders of the twelve tribes of the Children of Israel so that they could have further copies made as appeared appropriate to them, but without their having the right to add or subtract even a word.

In the following we read some verses of the *Holy Torah* (The Book of *Deuteronomy*):

Chapter 31

9: And Moses wrote this law and delivered it unto the priests the sons of Levi the bearers of the ark of the covenant the Lord, and unto all the elders of Israel.

12-13: Gather the people together, men, and women and children, and thy stranger that is within thy gates, that they may hear, and that they may learn, and fear the Lord your God and observe to do all the words of this law; and that their children, which have not known any thing, may hear and learn to fear the Lord your God, as long as ye live in the land which ye go over the Jordan to possess.

24: And it came to pass, when Moses had made an end of writing the words of this law in a book, until they were finished.

25: That Moses commanded the Levites, who bore the Ark of the Covenant of the Lord.

26: Take this book of the law, and put it in the side of the Ark of the Covenant of the Lord your God that it may be there as a witness for thee.

Chapter 22

25-26: But if a man find a betrothed damsel in the field, and the man doth force her and lie with her, then the man only that lay shall die; but unto the damsel thou shall do nothing; there is in the damsel no sin worthy of death; for as when a man riseth against his neighbour and slaveth him, even so is this matter: for he found her in the field, and the betrothed damsel cried, and there was none to save her.

Chapter Seven

•

Jerusalem and Palestine

Acquaintance with Jerusalem

The name of Jerusalem is mentioned six hundred and fifty seven times in the Jewish Bible. Although Jerusalem means The City of Peace, it was involved in forty wars in the short period from the Prophet David to the Dayans. Jerusalem has been sacked seventeen times and has twelve times passed from the hands of the followers of one religion to those of another. For three hundred years the Children of Israel were at war with powerful conquerors such as Greece and Rome. At the time of the Maccabee insurrection against the Greek rulers of the country the number of Jews who were hanged, usually from trees, exceeded the number of trees in the city. In the year 70 C.E. the Roman Gershon Titus, and in 135 C.E., King Hadrian, set Jerusalem on fire and destroyed it. The Romans wanted to cause this city – which had always been in the forefront of the affray against idol worshipping and polytheism – to vanish.

In 326 C.E., at the time when the Eastern Roman Empire ruled from Constantinople, the Church of the Holy Tomb was founded and Jerusalem was changed to a Christian city. There was a small number of Jews living there, but they were so poor that even the authorities recognized that they could not pay any taxes. Hieronymus (Born Eusebius Hieronymus Sophronius. Known as Bishop Sophronius. Lived 340-420 C.E.) wrote in detail about the difficult and miserable life of the Jews in Jerusalem at that time. Moslems captured Jerusalem in 638 C.E. Following the commands of the *Gracious Koran* and the traditions established by the Prophet Mohammed, the Moslems, during the 450 years that they controlled Jerusalem, entertained friendly relations with nations that possessed a Holy Book (Jews and Christians).

Abdolmalek Marvan founded the Ghobat Al-Sakhreh (Dome of Rock) on the exact spot where the Temple of Solomon had stood. In 1099 C.E., the Crusaders captured Jerusalem and ruled there for 88 years – a period during which they massacred many Jews and Moslems. After the expulsion of the Crusaders and the capture of Jerusalem by Salaheddin Ayoubi in 1187 C.E., different nations and governments ruled in Jerusalem, but it never became the capital city of an Islamic or Arabic country because of its lack of social and economic importance.

From 1517 to 1917, Jerusalem was governed by the Turks whose Ottoman Empire grew and developed during that period. Sultan Soleiman Ottomani rebuilt the walls of the city. During his reign he preserved friendly relations with the Jews and the Christians, based on the teachings of Islam. Sultan Soleiman died in 1566 C.E., but Palestine and Syria remained under Ottoman rule until 1917.

The immigration of the Jews to Jerusalem started in 1880. In 1898, Theodor Herzl, the founder of modern Zionism, visited Jerusalem. It was then a poor city with many parts in ruins – two thousand years of oppression were palpably in the air. In 1917, the English General, Allenby, freed Jerusalem from the hands of the Turks.

At present there are eighty mosques, eight hundred synagogues and two hundred churches in Jerusalem. The entire Holy area is one square kilometer and contains *interalia* the Wailing Wall, the Church of the Holy Sepulchre, the Heram Sharif with the Mosques of Omar and Al Aqsa, and much more. The population of Jerusalem has developed over the years as follows:

Year	Population	Jews	Moslems	Christians
1840	12900	5000	4600	3300
1870	22000	11000	6500	4500
1917	60800	30000	15000	15800
1948	149000	84000	40000	25000

Taking a Look at the History of Jerusalem

The Prophet Solomon founded Jerusalem in 960 B.C.E. It was a place for worshipping and offering sacrifices at the altar in the Holy Temple (Beit-Al-Moghaddas). In 586 B.C.E. Nebuchadnezzar, king of Babylon, conquered Palestine and Jerusalem and wreaked widespread destruction. In 536 B.C.E., Cyrus the Great, king of the Achaemenian Dynasty in Persia, ordered Jerusalem to be rebuilt. After twenty years, the Temple of Solomon was rebuilt by the king's generosity and mercy. Here was the holiest place of worship and for the offering of sacrifices for the Children of Israel. The Roman Emperor Titus again destroyed it, and only one of its walls was left standing – the Wailing Wall. This place is the holiest site for the Jews, which is still called Beit Hamigdash in Hebrew: Beit Al-Moghaddas in Arabic.

After the first destruction of Jerusalem by Nebuchadnezzar many of its Jewish inhabitants were taken away as captives to Babylon. Little by little these captives were scattered all around the world, up to the borders of China as well as north and west of Persia. Wherever they were they remained faithful to their religion and took their *Torah* scrolls with them.

Palestine was in the hands of Christians from 325 to 638 C.E. In the latter year Moslem Arabs conquered the area and held it until they were, in turn, defeated by the Crusaders. These latter built the temple of Domini in the city. As we mentioned before, Abdolmalek Marvan, the Omavi Caliph and his son

Walid built the Ghobbat Al-Sakhreh on the temple site. In fact, there had not been a mosque in this place prior to 691.

Al-Aqsa Mosque

The Moslems captured Palestine in 638 when the local Arab population was yet to be converted to the Moslem religion, the Prophet Mohammed having died in 632 prior to the conquest. Evidently, there had been no mosques in the area before then. As it is mentioned above, Ghobbat-Al-Sakhreh was built by Walid in 691.

Since the conquest of Jerusalem by the Moslems occurred in 638, and at that time, as well as thereafter until 691, not a single mosque existed in Jerusalem, and also the Ascension of the Prophet Mohammed (the Meraj) took place a year before the Hejira (620), it can be said that Ghobbat-Al-Sakhreh is not Al-Aqsa Mosque. The place, which has always been called Beit Al-Moghaddas (from the Hebrew term Beit-Hamigdash (the Holy Temple) has not been mentioned in the Meraj Verses. It is logical to conclude that the Al-Aqsa Mosque could not have existed at this place at the time of the Ascension of the Prophet Mohammed.

Ayoubian from 1187 to 1229, Mameloukian from 1260 until 1517, and Ottoman from 1517 to the 20th century during which time Palestine was part of Syria under Turkish rule; all ruled the country. As I have already said, after the sackings of Jerusalem by Nebuchadnezzar, and later by the Romans in 70 C.E., most Jews were dispersed to many countries, including Egypt (especially Alexandria), Italy (especially Rome) to many other European countries, but also to the countries in the vicinity of Palestine, including Persia (Iran). Until 1948, the year of the founding of the Jewish state, the Jews had spent 2,000 years in the Diaspora under conditions of suffering, humiliation and enforced rootlessness.

The *Koran* and Jerusalem

The name of Jerusalem has not been mentioned in the *Gracious Koran*. Only in *Sura Al-Osara*, in the first and second verses, the Almighty God says: :

Glory be to Him Who made His servant to go on a night from the Sacred Mosque to the remote mosque of which We have blessed the precincts, so that We may show to him some of Our signs; surely He is the Hearing, the Seeing.	سُبْحَانَ الَّذِي أَسْرَى بِعَبْدِهِ لَيْلًا مِنَ الْمَسْجِدِ الْحَرَامِ إِلَى الْمَسْجِدِ الْأَقْصَا الَّذِي بَرَكْنَا حَوْلَهُ لِنُرِيَهُ مِنْ آيَاتِنَا إِنَّهُ هُوَ السَّمِيعُ الْبَصِيرُ
And We gave Musa the Book and made it a guidance to the children of Israel, saying: Do not take a protector besides Me;	وَآتَيْنَا مُوسَى الْكِتَابَ وَجَعَلْنَاهُ هُدًى لِبَنِي إِسْرَائِيلَ أَلَّا تَتَّخِذُوا مِنْ دُونِي وَكِيلًا

We also read in *Sura Al-Araf 161*:

> And when it was said to them: Reside in this town and eat from it wherever you wish, and say: Put down from us our heavy burdens; and enter the gate making obeisance, We will forgive you your wrongs: We will give more to those who do good (to others).

وَإِذْ قِيلَ لَهُمُ اسْكُنُوا هَذِهِ الْقَرْيَةَ وَكُلُوا مِنْهَا حَيْثُ شِئْتُمْ وَقُولُوا حِطَّةٌ وَادْخُلُوا الْبَابَ سُجَّدًا نَغْفِرْ لَكُمْ خَطِيئَاتِكُمْ سَنَزِيدُ الْمُحْسِنِينَ

This shows that Jerusalem has been the place of worship for the Jews. In *Sura Al-Maidah 6* we read:

> O you who believe! when you rise up to prayer, wash your faces and your hands as far as the elbows, and wipe your heads and your feet to the ankles; and if you are under an obligation to perform a total ablution, then wash (yourselves) and if you are sick or on a journey, or one of you come from the privy, or you have touched the women, and you cannot find water, betake yourselves to pure earth and wipe your faces and your hands therewith, Allah does not desire to put on you any difficulty, but He wishes to purify you and that He may complete His favor on you, so that you may be grateful.

يَا أَيُّهَا الَّذِينَ آمَنُوا إِذَا قُمْتُمْ إِلَى الصَّلَاةِ فَاغْسِلُوا وُجُوهَكُمْ وَأَيْدِيَكُمْ إِلَى الْمَرَافِقِ وَامْسَحُوا بِرُءُوسِكُمْ وَأَرْجُلَكُمْ إِلَى الْكَعْبَيْنِ وَإِنْ كُنْتُمْ جُنُبًا فَاطَّهَّرُوا وَإِنْ كُنْتُمْ مَرْضَى أَوْ عَلَى سَفَرٍ أَوْ جَاءَ أَحَدٌ مِنْكُمْ مِنَ الْغَائِطِ أَوْ لَامَسْتُمُ النِّسَاءَ فَلَمْ تَجِدُوا مَاءً فَتَيَمَّمُوا صَعِيدًا طَيِّبًا فَامْسَحُوا بِوُجُوهِكُمْ وَأَيْدِيكُمْ مِنْهُ مَا يُرِيدُ اللَّهُ لِيَجْعَلَ عَلَيْكُمْ مِنْ حَرَجٍ وَلَكِنْ يُرِيدُ لِيُطَهِّرَكُمْ وَلِيُتِمَّ نِعْمَتَهُ عَلَيْكُمْ لَعَلَّكُمْ تَشْكُرُونَ

In *Sura Al-Osara 104*, a verse about the ascension of the Prophet Mohammed, we read:

> And We said to the Israelites after him: Dwell in the land: and when the promise of the next life shall come to pass, we will bring you both together in judgment.

وَقُلْنَا مِنْ بَعْدِهِ لِبَنِي إِسْرَائِيلَ اسْكُنُوا الْأَرْضَ فَإِذَا جَاءَ وَعْدُ الْآخِرَةِ جِئْنَا بِكُمْ لَفِيفًا

The Prophet Moses, after the departure of his people from Egypt ordered a big tent for his followers to pray in. The tent was called the Mishkan, which is broadly explained in the *Holy Torah*.

Jerusalem, the city of peace, will always be deep in my heart. I wish the city always to be a place for peace and friendship, especially for Christians, Moslems and Jews, who shall live with each other without violence and spitefulness. Jerusalem has always been a centre for mutual interests, holiness and respect for the followers of three great religions. I wish its inhabitants will live together peacefully, in mutual respect, without permitting political differences to damage its peace or deter humane behaviour. I pray that ultimately peace will prevail, putting an end to conflict and paving the road to the happiness of future generations. It is a pity that not even one verse in the *Holy Koran* has been dedicated to the holiness of Jerusalem.

The Deliverance of the Children of Israel and their Arrival in Canaan

I have previously referred to *Sura Al-Baqarah 47-48* when discussing the kindness of Almighty God to the Children of Israel in releasing them from the oppression of the Pharaoh. I will now cite some parts of the commentary written by the late Hassan-Ali Rashed on *Sura Al-Baqarah*:

> Concerning Verses 47 and 48 we have mentioned that there are many verses in the *Gracious Koran* that make reference to the Children of Israel, their beliefs and their heavenly book, but these matters are not described as extensively as they are in the *Torah*. There the events are described in detail and in their proper historical context, but the *Gracious Koran*, in addition to narrating historical occurrences, had three purposes in mentioning these events:
>
> The first purpose was to convince the Children of Israel in Medina, and especially those groups that opposed the Prophet Mohammed, to refrain from deviation and tread a straight path, by enabling them to rely on their own Prophet as he was quoted in their own book.
>
> The second purpose was to calm those who opposed the Prophet Mohammed, by showing some similarity with the Prophet Moses, so that they could believe him.
>
> The third purpose was to provide advice to the Moslems and others (who were prepared to accept advice).

By means of the interpretation of these verses and some others we can understand that Israel had not been a great nation from the beginning; in fact the change happened with the appearance of Abraham, who was an honest man and a true believer, and later on Joseph, another honest man who caused his nation to go to Egypt and to reside in that developed country. After the death of Joseph his people, fascinated by the life of luxury of the Egyptians, gradually lost their modesty, forgot their way of worshipping God, and started to copy the way of life of the local population, including the making and worshipping of idols. As a result, in the desert, when the Prophet Moses retired to the mountain for prayers, the people made a golden calf, as the Egyptians used to do. The people of Israel, being offspring of Abraham, were expected to be innovators and not imitators. However, already in Egypt, the Egyptians saw the Children of Israel as having become debased, without dignity, and hence they were considered as slaves and were maltreated and humiliated. These difficult times only ended when the Almighty God had mercy on the Children of Israel and sent the Prophet Moses to save them from the oppression of Pharaoh.

CHAPTER SEVEN

Moses saved the Children of Israel by leading them through the Red Sea without mishap. He kept them in the desert for 40 years (as mentioned in the *Holy Torah*) in order that they might become physically, morally and mentally strong, and recover from the tortures of Pharaoh and the consequent decline in their morale. Their long stay in the desert caused them to become accustomed to a simple life, to forget the luxuries of the Egyptian cities and to develop strong beliefs and the capacity for thinking sublime thoughts. When the Children of Israel conveyed to Moses that they found life in the desert to be monotonous, he replied to them, 'You should go to a city in which there are the blessings you like.' The Prophet Moses evidently meant to refer to Jerusalem, which had belonged to their ancestors and which, at that time, was under the sway of tribes, whose names are mentioned in the *Holy Torah*, which had captured the city and its suburbs.

After the death of Moses, the Children of Israel under the leadership of Yoshua ben Nun, regained Jerusalem and its suburbs and lived there honourably for many years. Afterwards, the 12 tribes had each been allocated a territory of its own. Unfortunately, over the years the urban atmosphere again caused the Children of Israel to become spoiled, with characteristics like greed, ambition and the desire for luxury becoming predominant, and thus they distanced themselves from the Almighty God's teachings.

Palestine and the Arabs

The Arabs conquered Jerusalem in 638. In 640 all the territory of Sham (Damascus) was captured by Moslems. Prior to that, there had not been any Moslems or mosques in Jerusalem or Palestine. Before the year 641 ended Moslems had conquered Iran and Egypt. The Bishop Sophronius, who was in charge of religious affairs in Jerusalem, agreed to surrender the city provided that the Caliph personally would come to Jerusalem to sign the treaty. Omar agreed to the condition and traveled to Medina with a simplicity that was more magnificent than glory. He had taken with him a bale of oats, a bag of dates, a water vessel and a wooden bowl. When Omar saw Khaled, Abu-Obeydeh and other corps commanders who had come to welcome him in sumptuous dresses, riding horses with golden laces, he was angry and threw a handful of pebbles at them, and berated them for enjoying excessive luxury. He negotiated moderately with Sophronius. Omar imposed low tributes on the defeated people and did not oppose the church. According to the historians, he even walked in Jerusalem accompanied by Sophronius, and when he heard that the inhabitants of Medina were worried that Omar would declare Jerusalem to be the capital of Islam, he hurried back to his small capital city. The Mosque of Omar was build later, in 691-694. It cannot be the Al-Aqsa Mosque.

Chapter Eight

The Changing of *Kibla*

The Veneration for Jerusalem

Until the second year of the *Hejira*, the Prophet Mohammed and his followers used to turn towards Jerusalem while praying. At the end of the second year of the Hejira, the Almighty God commanded that the *Kibla* (Object of Worship) be changed forthwith from being Jerusalem to being the Kaaba.

Moslems honour and respect Jerusalem because the Almighty God sent the Prophet Mohammed from Kaaba to Jerusalem by night, and from there to the kingdom of heaven. The ascension of the Prophet Mohammed began in Jerusalem. The other reason for the importance of Jerusalem for Moslems is that it used to be the *Kibla* of the Moslems until the second year of the *Hejira*.

It must be mentioned that Jerusalem has been the *Kibla* of the Children of Israel from the very beginning and remains so until today. Moslems greatly respect their first *Kibla*. Jerusalem is the birthplace of some of the Almighty God's prophets, and others visited it. In the eyes of the followers of the three great monotheistic religions (Judaism, Christianity, Islam) Jerusalem is seen as central to their beliefs and is regarded with veneration.

The ascension of Mohammed took place a year before the *Hejira* from Mecca to Medina. We read in the first verse of *Sura Al-Osara* as follows:

Glory be to Him Who made His servant to go on a night from the Sacred Mosque to the remote mosque of which We have blessed the precincts, so that We may show to him some of Our signs; surely He is the Hearing, the Seeing.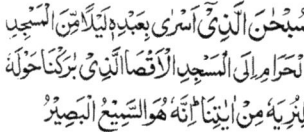

Immediately after this verse, the Almighty God speaks about the *Torah* and its role in the guidance given to the Children of Israel. He orders the Children of Israel not to rely on any help other than that provided by the Almighty God.

And We gave Musa the Book and made it a guidance to the children of Israel, saying: Do not take a protector besides Me;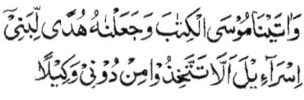

Al-Osara 2

When interpreting this verse we come to the conclusion that the monotheistic Jews do not recognize 'Ozar' as the son of God, and that the *Torah* of the

Children of Israel is, nevertheless, accepted as valid by the *Gracious Koran*. Every religion granted by the Almighty God is intended to provide guidance for human beings and is based on divine revelation. That is the reason why the virtuous worshippers of Almighty God and the believers of the Ibrahimian religions are saved both in this world and the next.

In Islam every religion is respected and all prophets sent by the Almighty God are accepted and regarded with reverence. The Almighty God promulgated the *Gracious Koran* as the source of endorsement of the *Holy Torah*. In Islam, which is the last and most complete monotheistic religion, some parts of the heavenly laws brought to the Children of Israel by the Prophet Moses have been adopted. Of these, some have been mentioned with changes, others without any change.

According to the *Gracious Koran*, being admitted to Paradise will reward a person who believe in the Almighty God and is stable in his belief.

Surely those who say, Our Lord is Allah, then they continue on the right way, they shall have no fear nor shall they grieve.

These are the dwellers of the garden, abiding therein: a reward for what they did.

Al-Ahqaf 13-14

Why was the *Kibla* Changed?

One of the important things, which the Prophet Mohammed did, was to change the *Kibla* from Jerusalem to Kaaba. As a consequence of this change, the ignorant Arabs, who believed in Kaaba, *Kibla* and pilgrimage, surrendered to the Prophet Mohammed and embraced Islam without resistance or bloodshed.

Before being changed by the Prophet Mohammed, Kaaba was a place for idolators, which was visited by people who used to go to Mecca on pilgrimage. At that time the Prophet Mohammed was under pressure from his uncles, as well from idolaters and Munafiqun, to return to his ancestral faith. These pressures probably caused doubt among some of the Children of Israel.

Before the onset of misunderstandings the Children of Israel had good relations with the Prophet Mohammed. They welcomed his 'Hijera' and cooperated with him in the religious wars. Friendly relations existed between the wives of the Prophet Mohammed and the Jewish women. Jews always prayed for his victory in the wars conducted by the Prophet Mohammed.

Since the Prophet Mohammed was chosen from among Arabs (*Al-Baqarah 51*) Kaaba was chosen instead of Jerusalem as the *Kibla* for Moslems in order to honour the tribes, which used to go to Kaaba on pilgrimage.

Moslems believe that one of the principal reasons for changing the *Kibla*

THE CHANGING OF *KIBLA*

was to cleanse the house of the Almighty God of the Munafiqun and the pagans. Thus Kaaba has been an important place, according to the command of the Almighty God, under social and economic aspects, in addition to the purely religious aspect. In the *Sura Al-Taubah 28*, stress is laid on the economical and commercial aspects.

O you who believe! the idolaters are nothing but unclean, so they shall not approach the Sacred Mosque after this year; and if you fear poverty then Allah will enrich you out of His grace if He please; surely Allah is Knowing, Wise.

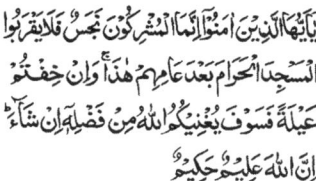

This verse was written appositely concerning the pilgrimage to Kaaba. It contains a prohibition against the entry of pagans, who were defined as being unclean and impure, into Masjid Al-Haram. This prohibition was justified and called for in order to avoid that the Kaaba continue to serve as a place of pilgrimage for idol worshippers.

Some Jews said 'The prophet we have been waiting for is not the Prophet Mohammed'. They based themselves on the *Holy Torah* and the *New Testament* when debating with Moslems about the *Gracious Koran*. Finally, the Arabs understood that, according to the *Gracious Koran*, they are a different nation from that of the Jews, with different *Kiblas*.

Kaaba, the *Kibla* of Moslems

The Prophet Mohammed succeeded, in a revolutionary manner, to change the tradition of idol worshipping to one of worshipping a single God – monotheism – although this was completely contrary to the previously prevailing customs. This fundamental transformation and the drastic change in values it implied took place in such a way that the Arabs did not feel any wrench from their past. On the contrary, they felt revived and uplifted with their new symbols of sanctity. The Prophet Mohammed accomplished the whole process of transmutation from paganism to monotheism much faster and more suddenly than any mental or cultural revolution. It may be said that the revolution wrought by the Prophet Mohammed was an inter-cultural change, which preserved the improved traditional background.

The Revolt of Abdallah Zobair in Mecca

At the beginning, Abdolmalek Marvan decided to resolve the conflict with the Romans. For this purpose he was prepared to bear heavy burdens. After having

CHAPTER EIGHT

completed his ventures against the foreign enemies he planned to crush the son of Zobair, and he engaged in both the military and political aspects of the fight for defeating the ruler of Hijaz. In order to prevent the pilgrims being influenced by the son of Zobair and being called to his colours, Abdolmalek Marvan forbade the people of Damascus to go to Mecca on the Hajj pilgrimage.

Yaghoubi writes: 'People complained of being prevented from going to Mecca on pilgrimage. Abdolmalek replied that this was due to the fact that Ibn Shohab Zahri had recited the injunction of the Prophet Mohammed to go on pilgrimage to three mosques, namely Masjid-Al-Haram, his mosque and the mosque in Jerusalem. Abdolmalek continued: "Today Jerusalem is as honourable as Masjid-Al-Haram for you". According to Ibn Shohab, the rock on which the Jews used to offer sacrifices was the same rock that the Prophet Mohammed stepped on at the time of his ascension.'

Abdolmalek ordered a *kibla* to be laid down around the rock and to have it embellished with silk curtains. His real purpose was to prevent Mecca and Medina from flourishing and to strengthen the position of Damascus as a sanctuary in the eyes of the Moslems. (Other leaders tried this again later). To attain his aim, Abdolmalek sent his army to Iraq in order to overthrow Moasseb, son of the Zobair, who was the ruler of Basra and Koofa. He enlisted support from some of the Iraqi leaders by making them promises. Finally, Moasseb was killed (in the year 71 C.E.); his army was defeated and the Iraqi issue was resolved. Then came the time of the Hijaz! Abdolmalek sent Hajaj Ibn Youssef to Hijaz. He surrounded Mecca and destroyed the city, including its House of God by the use of his siege equipment, which included catapults. In this war Abdallah fought bravely, although abandoned by his companions, and was finally killed. With his death, the last of Abdolmalek was eliminated (73 C.E.).

Abdallah, whose corpse was hanged by Hajaj, was described as a virtuous man who had stood up against three former caliphates. He was castigated in some poems and legends, but the aspersions cast there are not true. In this campaign Hajaj did everything he could to dishonour his enemies. He not only sacked the Kaaba and ravished the prophet's tomb, pulpit and mosque, but he also bestowed honours on some of his companions, such as Abdallah Ansari and Ens Ibn Malek Saedi, for having killed Ottomans.

Kaaba in the *Gracious Koran*

The *Gracious Koran* says that the Almighty God is everywhere and can be felt by human beings irrespective of the direction in which they are facing – *Sura Al-Baqarah 115*.

And Allah's is the East and the West, therefore, whither you turn, thither is Allah's purpose; surely Allah is Ample-giving, Knowing.

وَلِلَّهِ الْمَشْرِقُ وَالْمَغْرِبُ فَأَيْنَمَا تُوَلُّوا فَثَمَّ وَجْهُ اللَّهِ إِنَّ اللَّهَ وَاسِعٌ عَلِيمٌ

THE CHANGING OF KIBLA

But people have always respected the Kaaba, as the first house of God, since the time of its founder, Ebrahim Khalil.

Most surely the first house appointed for men is the one at Bekka, blessed and a guidance for the nations.

In it are clear signs, the standing place of Ibrahim, and whoever enters it shall be secure, and pilgrimage to the House is incumbent upon men for the sake of Allah, (upon) every one who is able to undertake the journey to it; and whoever disbelieves, then surely Allah is Self-sufficient, above any need of the worlds.

إِنَّ أَوَّلَ بَيْتٍ وُضِعَ لِلنَّاسِ لَلَّذِي بِبَكَّةَ مُبَارَكًا وَهُدًى لِّلْعَالَمِينَ

فِيهِ آيَاتٌ بَيِّنَاتٌ مَّقَامُ إِبْرَاهِيمَ وَمَن دَخَلَهُ كَانَ آمِنًا وَلِلَّهِ عَلَى النَّاسِ حِجُّ الْبَيْتِ مَنِ اسْتَطَاعَ إِلَيْهِ سَبِيلًا وَمَن كَفَرَ فَإِنَّ اللَّهَ غَنِيٌّ عَنِ الْعَالَمِينَ

Al-Imran 96-97

The repair of the House of God, which is referred to in the subsequent verse as 'The First House of God', emphasizes the dignity and importance of Islam and the *Koran* for the people.

According to the *Gracious Koran*, Moslems must turn in the direction of the Majid Al-Haram for their daily prayers. Besides, Moslems also believe that one should turn towards the Majid Al-Haram (Kaaba) when meditating, teaching and learning science, in order that these activities may be blessed. It is an absolute obligation for Moslems to turn towards the Kaaba and recite 'In the name of God, the merciful and compassionate', when slaughtering animals which are clean and lawful to be eaten. In general, *Kibla* is seen as a source of blessings, and it is sinful to dishonour it.

Chapter Nine

•

Jihad

Moslems believe that the *Gracious Koran* is righteous and that all its verses, commands and prohibitions are true and were sent to the Prophet Mohammed through Gabriel, the angel of celestial revelation.

This Holy Book, which is in fact the last heavenly book, contains eternal commands and laws that can be applied and put into practice in any era and at any time.

The author believes that these beliefs are true. I will now discuss the verse in which there are clear references to the *Jihad* – which, strictly speaking, means endeavor, struggle or fight, but idiomatically has assumed the meaning of the Holy War.

Philosophy of the *Jihad*

It has at all times been a compulsory and inevitable duty of Moslems to defend the principles of Islam. Whenever strangers or atheists threatened Moslems, the leaders of the Islamic society would issue orders for a *Jihad* in order to defend their followers' lives, residences, faith, honour and dignity. Obviously, the *Jihad* should not be misused to settle local differences, to sustain personal tastes, or defend individual or social interests.

In our times we have witnessed many events involving the shedding of blood among Moslems. Unfortunately, today we see that many motives are adduced for the shedding of blood, the reason often being mere futile excuses, or a narrow group of sectional interests.

Imam Ali and His Abstention from Fighting Wars and Shedding Blood

Imam Ali was always fond of deliberate discussions, reasoning, offering guidance and giving advice, and preferred to abstain from conducting wars or battles and shedding blood. It was his custom to address his soldiers and commanders accordingly, endeavoring to convince them to share his views.

Imam Ali, who was the leader of the Shiites and the fourth Caliph of the Moslems, made great efforts to dissuade the opposing sides from engaging in the wars of 'Jamal', 'Saffein', and 'Nakassin'; and he tried to delay the breaking out of the 'Nakathin', 'Ghassetin', and 'Mareghin' wars. His interests were of a spiritual kind. He was not interested in the governorship, and he exerted himself mainly to ensure the continuity of Islam, the uninterrupted validity of the *Koran*, and the application of the Islamic laws.

Before the beginning of the 'Jamal' war, Imam Ali ordered his soldiers not to be the initiators of war, not to kill the wounded, pursue the defeated enemies or abuse their corpses, not to enter their houses, violate their women or steal their property. (*Nahj-Al-Balagheh*).

In order to become familiar with the nature of *Jihad* we find it opportune to include here an outline of some parts of the learned essays of Shahid Mortaza Mottahari:

> It is important to clarify the accurate nature of the *Jihad* according to Islam, and thus become aware of the truth in this regard.
>
> The unanimous view of researchers on the subject is that the nature of *Jihad* is defensive; and they are in full agreement on the view that Islam does not permit the initiation of war or killing for the purpose of aggression, accumulating wealth, gathering human resources such as families, wives, servants etc., or deriving any other economic benefit by depriving the opposing side of it. Islam considers wars that have such objectives as being cruel, and not within the permitted scope of defensive wars against oppressors.

Jihad in the *Gracious Koran*

The *Gracious Koran* itself is the best source for correctly understanding the *Jihad*, its opportuneness and range. Through understanding the verses of the *Gracious Koran* we will learn under what conditions and at which times a *Jihad* will be recognized as important, so that participating in it becomes the vital duty of every Moslem.

In *Sura Al-Baqarah 190* we read:

And fight in the way of Allah with those who fight with you, and do not exceed the limits, surely Allah does not love those who exceed the limits.	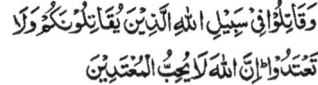

Wherever the word *Jihad* is mentioned in the *Gracious Koran*, Moslem believers are adjured to be just, fair, and moderate, and not to behave spitefully towards the defeated side. In *Sura Al-Muntahanah 7-9* we read:

It may be that Allah will bring about friendship between you and those whom you hold to be your enemies among them; and Allah is Powerful; and Allah is Forgiving, Merciful.	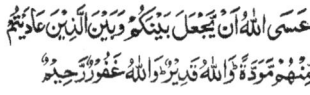

(continued next page)

It may be that Allah will bring about friendship between you and those whom you hold to be your enemies among them; and Allah is Powerful; and Allah is Forgiving, Merciful.

Allah does not forbid you respecting those who have not made war against you on account of (your) religion, and have not driven you forth from your homes, that you show them kindness and deal with them justly; surely Allah loves the doers of justice.

Allah only forbids you respecting those who made war upon you on account of (your) religion, and drove you forth from your homes and backed up (others) in your expulsion, that you make friends with them, and whoever makes friends with them, these are the unjust.

Chapter Ten

•

God's Angels

We have stated before that part of Islam is a firm belief in the sole God, the mission of the Prophet, the Day of Resurrection, and God's angels. It is necessary for Moslems to believe that the Prophet Mohammed is the last prophet.

For the Jews two angels, Gabriel and Michael, are the most holy and call for respect. Every Saturday night Jews recite prayers that demonstrate the respect the Children of Israel (Bene Yisrael) have for these angels.

Chapter Eleven

•

Verses of Reprimand

By carefully reading the verses of the *Koran* we will become aware that Mohammed is a true prophet, and that the verses of reprimand are mostly sent to awaken the believers and to warn them not to commit sins, as well as to punish the sinners. The Prophet Mohammed had foreseen that the most terrible crime in the history of human beings would be committed within his own family. The martyrdom of Imam Ali in the mosque at the time of prayer, and later the martyrdom of Imam Hossein and his family, involving, as it did, great cruelty, were in fact some of the most horrible crimes. It must be remembered that both were true Imams and great leaders of Islam. Every year more than 100 million Shi'ites commemorate these tragedies.

Here none of the interpreters refer in anyway to the offspring of Yasid, and yet they condemn the monotheist Jews of today for the sins their ancestors allegedly committed three or four thousand years ago. This interpretation, which pretends that the Moslems, and especially those who lived after the Prophet Mohammed, were innocent and pure as the driven snow, while the Jews were the only sinners in the world, really represents a capital offence in the holy religion of Islam.

The verses of reprimand are relevant to the pre-Islamic periods. In the *Gracious Koran*, God regarded the followers of religions with heavenly books as being independent in their religions and did not command them to convert to Islam. Thus we see that there was no need for so many verses on the subject to be sent to his messenger. The real reason why this was done was to persuade the Moslems to be pure (in contrast to the Jewish sinners) and to abstain from evil deeds. The aim was to bring about a change in a nation that was atheist and ignorant before the advent of Islam, to purify Moslems and prevail upon them to abstain from killings and committing other sins.

Unfortunately, as history has shown us, Moslems have mostly been quarrelling among themselves, defying the ideals of Islam. The war between Iran and Iraq, and the events in Afghanistan, are recent examples of this. The murder of Imam Ali, killing of the innocent grandchildren of the Prophet Mohammed, exemplify that sinfulness is not an exclusive trait of the Jews.

A Look at the Verses that Condemn Sinners

At that time the normal way of conducting negotiations was verbal, and the Prophet Mohammed employed the same method.

The visits of Prophet Mohammed to idol worshippers and the followers of other religions with a heavenly book were not mass meetings. Every time a limited number of people enjoyed the honour of meeting the Prophet and enjoyed his advice and blessings. His counsels and guidance saved the atheists and idol worshippers of that region, especially in Medina.

We must stress that the negotiations of the Prophet Mohammed with the Jews were also carried on according to the custom of the time – communicated verbally.

Evidence in the *Koran* About the Illiteracy of the Jews in Mecca and Medina

The verses of *Sura Al-Baqarah 77-79* clearly tell us about the illiteracy of the Jews of Mecca and Medina, and their ignorance concerning the *Holy Torah*:

Do they not know that Allah knows what they keep secret and what they make known?

أَوَلَا يَعْلَمُونَ أَنَّ اللَّهَ يَعْلَمُ مَا يُسِرُّونَ وَمَا يُعْلِنُونَ

Al-Baqarah 77

And there are among them illiterates who know not the Book but only lies, and they do but conjecture.

وَمِنْهُمْ أُمِّيُّونَ لَا يَعْلَمُونَ الْكِتَابَ إِلَّا أَمَانِيَّ وَإِنْ هُمْ إِلَّا يَظُنُّونَ

Al-Baqarah 78

Woe, then, to those who write the book with their hands and then say: This is from Allah, so that they may take for it a small price; therefore woe to them for what their hands have written and woe to them for what they earn.

فَوَيْلٌ لِلَّذِينَ يَكْتُبُونَ الْكِتَابَ بِأَيْدِيهِمْ ثُمَّ يَقُولُونَ هَٰذَا مِنْ عِنْدِ اللَّهِ لِيَشْتَرُوا بِهِ ثَمَنًا قَلِيلًا فَوَيْلٌ لَهُمْ مِمَّا كَتَبَتْ أَيْدِيهِمْ وَوَيْلٌ لَهُمْ مِمَّا يَكْسِبُونَ

Al-Baqarah 79

Although all the verses of reprimand are sent to warn all human beings not to commit sins at any time, it is not correct to apply the condemnation to all the Children of Israel. In fact, the Children of Israel were living at that time already in many parts of the world. They had synagogues in the big cities and complied with their religious duties. They may not even have been aware of the existence of the city of Medina and of the fact that there were some Jews living there. Hence, the sins and dishonesty of some Jews in Medina cannot forever be held against all the Jews wherever they may be living in the world! The verses of reprimand contain no reference to a geographical area other than the district of Hijaz. They were addressed to those whose behaviour was displayed before the Prophet Mohammed, in fact those who lived in his vicinity. The subjects of the fish, and of dishonouring the Sabbath and rejecting the *Holy Torah*, are clear evidence of this. It must be emphasized that the matter of the sinfulness and violence of the Jews that is mentioned in the *Gracious Koran* might even have referred to Jews who had lived in past times, especially at the time of the Prophet Moses.

The purpose of sending verses of reprimand was to condemn the sinners and to alert the believers lest they deviate from the right path and disobey their religious regulations. It is obvious that the Almighty God and the Prophet Mohammed knew perfectly well that not all the Jews were fishermen, and that not all the Jewish fishermen had committed sins. It can be said that the sending of the verses of reprimand about Jewish sinners shows the attention paid by the Almighty God to the Jewish religion and the believers of Judaism, as well as the respect shown to it and them by the Prophet Mohammed, even if Mohammed was upset by the disobedience and sinning of some of the Jews.

The Trustworthiness of the Follower of the Religions with a Heavenly Book

In *Sura Al-Imran*, the Almighty God says as follows:

He specially chooses for His mercy whom He pleases; and Allah is the Lord of mighty grace.

Al-Imran 74

And among the followers of the Book there are some such that if you entrust one (of them) with a heap of wealth, he shall pay it back to you; and among them there are some such that if you entrust one (of them) with a dinar he shall not pay it back to you except so long as you remain firm in demanding it; this is because they say: There is not upon us in the matter of the unlearned people any way (to reproach); and they tell a lie against Allah while they know.

Al-Imran 75

Yea, whoever fulfills his promise and guards (against evil)—then surely Allah loves those who guard (against evil).

Al-Imran 76

(As for) those who take a small price for the covenant of Allah and their own oaths—surely they shall have no portion in the hereafter, and Allah will not speak to them, nor will He look upon them on the day of resurrection nor will He purify them, and they shall have a painful chastisement.

Al-Imran 77

These verses are clear and self-evident; according to the Jewish religion. It is forbidden to use the property of others, especially property that was given in trust.

In the *Holy Torah* it is emphasized that property rights must be respected irrespective of the religion and other characteristics of the owner. These verses are addressed to all humankind, especially to the believers of religions with a heavenly book, so as to stress that they should not covet the property of others.

A Careful Analysis of the *Gracious Koran*'s Verses in Condemnation of Sinners

When we look at the verses of the *Gracious Koran* that are devoted to the condemnation of the Jewish sinners, we see that verses of 'fear' and 'hope' appear consecutively, i.e., wherever a verse contains condemnation it is followed by verses of sympathy and hopefulness. In fact the educational method of the *Gracious Koran* is based on the principle of 'Punishment and Reward'.

Surely those who believe, and those who are Jews, and the Christians, and the Sabians, whoever believes in Allah and the Last day and does good, they shall have their reward from their Lord, and there is no fear for them, nor shall they grieve.

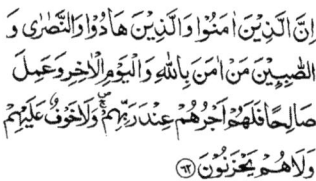

Al-Baqarah 62

This verse is repeated in the *Sura Al-Maidah 69*, which shows its importance:

A party of the followers of the Book desire that they should lead you astray, and they lead not astray but themselves, and they do not perceive.

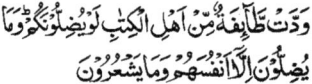

Human beings can really be saved and become happy, after having made great efforts and having passed along difficult paths. Clearly the Almighty God indicates the correct way to his subjects, but human beings are free to choose the course they wish to take.

And upon Allah it rests to show the right way, and there are some deviating (ways); and if He please He would certainly guide you all aright.

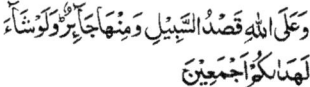

Al-Nahl 9

In another verse we see:

CHAPTER ELEVEN

> Whoever does good whether male or female and he is a believer, We will most certainly make him live a happy life, and We will most certainly give them their reward for the best of what they did.

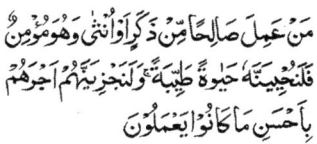

Al-Nahl 97

Quite clearly the weak and strong points of any group are closely correlated with the conditions ruling at any given moment in time and the place where they are domiciled at that time. This fact could be observed not only at the time of the beginning of Islam, but also today.

In *Sura Al-Taubah* the Almighty God refers to those who pretended to be believers in a religion with a heavenly book, while in actual fact they rejected the idea of the Day of Judgment and altogether did not adhere to any true religion. Thus they were actually to be considered to be 'Munafiqun', and were not to be regarded as Jews.

> Fight those who do not believe in Allah, nor in the latter day, nor do they prohibit what Allah and His Apostle have prohibited, nor follow the religion of truth, out of those who have been given the Book, until they pay the tax in acknowledgment of superiority and they are in a state of subjection.

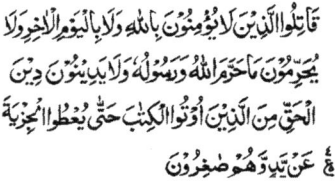

Al-Taubah 29

The object of the above verse is indubitably the 'Munafiqun', since the believers of religions with a heavenly book believe in the Almighty God and the Day of Judgment. The latter consider as unlawful whatever is prohibited by the Almighty God and his prophets. The 'Munafiqun', who were ignorant and illiterate idol worshippers, engaged in fights with them with the object of making them abjure their faith, but were vanquished in the end. They do not even exist anymore.

The Warning of the *Gracious Koran* about the Polytheists

In *Sura Al-Taubah* the Almighty God warns Moslems not to permit the polytheists to approach the Masjid Al-Haram, even if they thereby see reduction in their annual earnings and incur economic losses.

> O you who believe! the idolaters are nothing but unclean, so they shall not

(continued next page)

Verses of Reprimand

approach the Sacred Mosque after this year; and if you fear poverty then Allah will enrich you out of His grace if He please; surely Allah is Knowing, Wise.	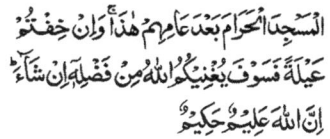

Al-Taubah 28

Idol Worshipping in Arabia Before the Advent of Islam

Most interpreters of the *Sura* of Oneness deal with the different idols that existed in the Era of Ignorance and the way they were worshipped. Bayzavi, the famous interpreter of the *Gracious Koran* of Iranian origin, has explained extensively the meaning of 'Samad' and concludes that human beings are unable to fathom the real nature of the Almighty God. According to Bayzavi, the phrase 'Lam Valad Va Lam Youlad' means 'He does not bear and is not born. Bayzavi believes that the purpose of sending this verse was to counter the beliefs the Arabs held at that time.

Before Islam, Arabs were idol worshippers. Many idols existed at the time, and the names of some of them have been preserved to this day. As the Arabs were illiterate they were unable to write history, and hence we do not know details of the way they prayed to their idols. Some of these were male, others female, and according to anecdotes they even used to marry and bear children. These beliefs of the Arabs bear a certain resemblance to those contained in the mythology of Greece and Babylon at the time.

Traces of polytheism can even be observed in some of the ideas held by people who considered themselves to be followers of a heavenly book.

And the Jews say: Uzair is the son of Allah; and the Christians say: The Messiah is the son of Allah; these are the words of their mouths; they imitate the saying of those who disbelieved before; may Allah destroy them; how they are turned away!	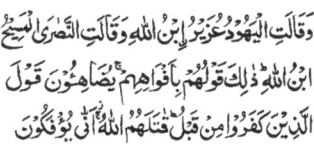

Al-Taubah 30

During his mission, the Prophet Mohammed used to address himself to ignorant people as well as to idol worshippers, all of whom held superstitious and false beliefs about the Almighty God and his angels. They believed that the Almighty God had a child called 'Ozair'. Some of these people represented themselves to be Jews, but in fact they were idol worshippers who angered the Almighty God, and who eventually vanished.

Judaism, which has been based on monotheism since the time of the Prophet Moses, has not developed any contrary concepts up to this day. It can confidently be expected that this situation will remain unchanged, also in the future because of the ways in which prayers and ceremonies are observed and handed down from one generation to another. In Jewish prayers the most important statement is the following: 'Oh Children of Israel Our God is the sole God'. Every observant Jew must repeat this statement twice a day, and it is written down and displayed in the home and the place of work, so that it is always remembered.

In the *Gracious Koran* there are verses referring to the trustworthiness and abstemiousness of the followers of religions with a heavenly book, and they are distanced from the oppressors, sinners and unbelievers. In *Sura Al-Imran 74* we read:

He specially chooses for His mercy whom He pleases; and Allah is the Lord of mighty grace.	

And then we read:

And among the followers of the Book there are some such that if you entrust one (of them) with a heap of wealth, he shall pay it back to you; and among them there are some such that if you entrust one (of them) with a dinar he shall not pay it back to you except so long as you remain firm in demanding it; this is because they say: There is not upon us in the matter of the unlearned people any way (to reproach); and they tell a lie against Allah while they know.

Al Imran 75

Emphasis on Respect for Property Rights of Others

According to the laws of the *Torah*, the property rights of every one must be respected irrespective of what his religious beliefs are. The true Jew respects the lives and property of others.

In the *Gracious Koran* we read:

Yea, whoever fulfills his promise and guards (against evil)—then surely Allah loves those who guard (against evil).	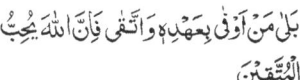

Al-Imran 76

The end of the oppressors, and rewards for good people, *Sura Al-Imran 113*:

They are not all alike; of the followers of the Book there is an upright party; they recite Allah's communications in the night time and they adore (Him).

According to the *Gracious Koran*, the true believers and abstemious people are those who persuade other to do good deeds, and prevent them from doing wrong.

> They believe in Allah and the last day, and they enjoin what is right and forbid the wrong, and they strive with one another in hastening to good deeds, and those are among the good.

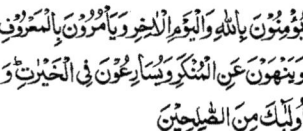

Al-Imran 114

It is, of course, obvious that the Almighty God will not ignore the good deeds of anybody.

> And whatever good they do, they shall not be denied it, and Allah knows those who guard (against evil).

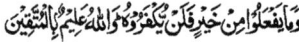

Al-Imran 115

The *Verses 113* and *115* contain warnings and admonitions to the oppressors who disobey the commands of the Almighty God.

Treatment of the Jews by the Prophets

Prophets are the only ones to bring messages from the Almighty God to human beings in order to save them and ensure that they should be happy in the two worlds. To calm the anxiety of the Prophet Mohammed concerning the difficult path ahead of him when propagating Islam, the Almighty God says (according to the *Gracious Koran*) as follows:

> Your Lord knows you best; He will have mercy on you if He pleases, or He will chastise you if He pleases; and We have not sent you as being in charge of them.

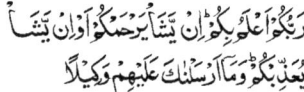

Al-Osara 54

The uncouth and irresponsible behaviour of some renegade Jews towards the Prophet Mohammed at the early stages of the dissemination of Islam should not be held against the Children of Israel generally, and does not justify labelling the majority of the Jews, who were true followers of a monotheist religion, as atheists and rebels. The *Gracious Koran* states that the followers of religions with a heavenly book are not uniform. Moslems who lived in Medina did not have any problems with the Jews. An agreement concluded between

CHAPTER ELEVEN

the Prophet Mohammed and the Jews in Medina was a basis for peaceful co-existence.

| And whatever Allah restored to His Apostle from them, you did not press forward against it any horse or a riding camel, but Allah gives authority to His apostles against whom He pleases, and Allah has power over all things. | وَمَآ أَفَآءَ اللّٰهُ عَلَىٰ رَسُولِهِ مِنْهُمْ فَمَآ أَوْجَفْتُمْ عَلَيْهِ مِنْ خَيْلٍ وَلَا رِكَابٍ وَلَٰكِنَّ اللّٰهَ يُسَلِّطُ رُسُلَهُ عَلَىٰ مَن يَشَآءُ وَاللّٰهُ عَلَىٰ كُلِّ شَىْءٍ قَدِيرٌ |

Al-Hashr 6

Although at the early stages of Islam, before the Prophet's government was fully established in the Arabian Peninsula, there had been some Jewish tribes who plotted and conspired against the Prophet Mohammad, yet there is no historical evidence to show that any attack was ever carried out by the Jews against the Moslems at this time; nor is there any record of any Moslem having been martyred by the Jews in the same period. The reason is that most Jews believed that the Prophet Mohammed had been sent to guide and save the atheists and idol worshippers, and this is confirmed in the mentioned verses.

In the Khandagh war, the Jews, as was usual at that time, cooperated with the Moslems in defending Medina against idol worshippers and atheists. The Moslems were in doubt as to whether the Jews would stand by them. What happened was that the Munaqfun deserted the Prophet Mohammed, but the Jews were faithful and remained to defend Medina, until the prophet dismissed them so that they could celebrate their Holy Sabbath.

It is legitimate to speculate that in the case of a victory of the idol worshippers in the war with the Moslems, the former would have continued to attack and kill the Jews, because of the agreement that was known to exist between the Jew and the Moslems. It can be said, contrary to rumours current at the time, that the Jews did not act against the Moslems, barring some individuals who were not of the mainstream of Judaism. The majority of Jews viewed Islam as a monotheistic religion that combated atheism.

Hesitations of Some Followers of Religions with a Heavenly Book

It is appropriate here to look at *Sura Al-Baqarah 145*, which is the greatest among the *Suras* of the *Gracious Koran*:

| And even if you bring to those who have been given the Book every sign they would not follow your qiblah, nor can you be a follower of their qiblah, neither are they the followers of each other's qiblah, and if you follow their desires after the knowledge that has come to you, then you shall most surely be among the unjust. | وَلَئِنْ أَتَيْتَ الَّذِينَ أُوتُوا الْكِتَابَ بِكُلِّ آيَةٍ مَّا تَبِعُوا قِبْلَتَكَ وَمَا أَنتَ بِتَابِعٍ قِبْلَتَهُمْ وَمَا بَعْضُهُم بِتَابِعٍ قِبْلَةَ بَعْضٍ وَلَئِنِ اتَّبَعْتَ أَهْوَاءَهُم مِّن بَعْدِ مَا جَاءَكَ مِنَ الْعِلْمِ إِنَّكَ إِذًا لَّمِنَ الظَّالِمِينَ |

This shows that the Prophet Mohammed recognized the true beliefs of the followers of religions with a heavenly book, as well as their different *Kiblas*.

The verses of reprimand are the signs of attention and kindness which the great Prophet of Islam bestowed upon the Children of Israel. He censured the behaviour of Jewish sinners and objected to their infractions and crimes. In other words, he wished that the Jews should behave according to the rules of their own heavenly book and that they abstain from intermingling with the atheists.

From Idol Worshipping to Monotheism

The Prophet Mohammed guided the ignorant and the atheists to monotheism. When it appeared that there was relatively strong opposition to the new creed, the Almighty God commanded his messenger to crush the existing powers in order to ease the spread of Islam. A few Jewish tribes were also among those who were destined to be eradicated.

It is important to remember that the purpose of these campaigns was never the rooting out of the religion. No church, synagogue or other holy places for Jews or Christians was ever destroyed. It should also be noted that the Children of Israel never were the aggressors, and in fact in the history of Islam there do not figure any martyrs whose death is ascribed to the Jews. In the course of time the Jews and their religion vanished from the Hijaz.

Children of Israel in the Hijaz

At the time of the rise of Islam there had been Jewish residents in tens of cities and villages in the Hijaz. In the course of time they either intermarried with the Moslems or were killed in clashes with militant Moslems, so that ultimately, none remained.

In general the Jews obeyed the local rulers and never represented a troublesome element, neither for their fellow citizens nor for the rulers. They even had a special prayer for the health and happiness of their fellow residents and rulers, which was recited together with other prayers in the synagogues on Saturdays. (This custom still exists to this day.)

The verses of the *Gracious Koran* do not contain any written alteration of the *Holy Torah*. Alterations in Holy Books were usually made at the instigation of the rulers, whatever their title, and were motivated by economic or political interests of the oppressors and renegades and were justified on spurious religious grounds. The true followers of the religion involved were never parties to such manoeuvres. The Jews believe to this day it has never been proved that the *Holy Torah* was altered in any way.

The *Holy Torah* was written down during the lifetime of the Prophet Moses,

CHAPTER ELEVEN

and its copies were entrusted to Yoshua ben Nun, the successor of the Prophet Moses.

In the following *Suras* of the *Gracious Koran* the Almighty God has cited some verses of the *Holy Torah* on the subject of distinguishing between permissible and forbidden deeds, and on the subject of just judgments:

(They are) listeners of a lie, devourers of what is forbidden; therefore if they come to you, judge between them or turn aside from them, and if you turn aside from them, they shall not harm you in any way; and if you judge, judge between them with equity; surely Allah loves those who judge equitably.

سَمَّاعُونَ لِلْكَذِبِ أَكَّالُونَ لِلسُّحْتِ فَإِنْ جَاءُوكَ فَاحْكُمْ بَيْنَهُمْ أَوْ أَعْرِضْ عَنْهُمْ وَإِنْ تُعْرِضْ عَنْهُمْ فَلَنْ يَضُرُّوكَ شَيْئًا وَإِنْ حَكَمْتَ فَاحْكُمْ بَيْنَهُمْ بِالْقِسْطِ إِنَّ اللَّهَ يُحِبُّ الْمُقْسِطِينَ

Al-Maidah 42

And how do they make you a judge and they have the Tavrat wherein is Allah's judgment? Yet they turn back after that, and these are not the believers.

وَكَيْفَ يُحَكِّمُونَكَ وَعِنْدَهُمُ التَّوْرَاةُ فِيهَا حُكْمُ اللَّهِ ثُمَّ يَتَوَلَّوْنَ مِنْ بَعْدِ ذَلِكَ وَمَا أُولَئِكَ بِالْمُؤْمِنِينَ

Al-Maidah 43

And We sent after them in their footsteps Isa, son of Marium, verifying what was before him of the Tavrat and We gave him the Injeel in which was guidance and light, and verifying what was before it of Tavrat and a guidance and an admonition for those who guard (against evil).

وَقَفَّيْنَا عَلَى آثَارِهِمْ بِعِيسَى ابْنِ مَرْيَمَ مُصَدِّقًا لِمَا بَيْنَ يَدَيْهِ مِنَ التَّوْرَاةِ وَآتَيْنَاهُ الْإِنْجِيلَ فِيهِ هُدًى وَنُورٌ وَمُصَدِّقًا لِمَا بَيْنَ يَدَيْهِ مِنَ التَّوْرَاةِ وَهُدًى وَمَوْعِظَةً لِلْمُتَّقِينَ

Al-Maidah 46

And the followers of the Injeel should have judged by what Allah revealed in it; and whoever did not judge by what Allah revealed, those are they that are the transgressors.

وَلْيَحْكُمْ أَهْلُ الْإِنْجِيلِ بِمَا أَنْزَلَ اللَّهُ فِيهِ وَمَنْ لَمْ يَحْكُمْ بِمَا أَنْزَلَ اللَّهُ فَأُولَئِكَ هُمُ الْفَاسِقُونَ

Al-Maidah 47

And We have revealed to you the Book with the truth, verifying what is before it of the Book and a guardian over it, therefore judge between them by what Allah has revealed, and do not follow their low desires (to turn away) from the truth that has come to you; for every one of you did We appoint a law and a way, and if Allah had pleased He would have made

وَأَنْزَلْنَا إِلَيْكَ الْكِتَابَ بِالْحَقِّ مُصَدِّقًا لِمَا بَيْنَ يَدَيْهِ مِنَ الْكِتَابِ وَمُهَيْمِنًا عَلَيْهِ فَاحْكُمْ بَيْنَهُمْ بِمَا أَنْزَلَ اللَّهُ وَلَا تَتَّبِعْ أَهْوَاءَهُمْ عَمَّا جَاءَكَ مِنَ الْحَقِّ لِكُلٍّ جَعَلْنَا مِنْكُمْ شِرْعَةً وَمِنْهَاجًا وَلَوْ شَاءَ اللَّهُ

(continued next page)

you (all) a single people, but that He might try you in what He gave you, therefore strive with one another to hasten to virtuous deeds; to Allah is your return, of all (of you), so He will let you know that in which you differed;

لَجَعَلَكُمْ أُمَّةً وَاحِدَةً وَلَٰكِن لِّيَبْلُوَكُمْ فِى مَاۤ ءَاتَىٰكُمْ فَٱسْتَبِقُوا۟ ٱلْخَيْرَٰتِ إِلَى ٱللَّهِ مَرْجِعُكُمْ جَمِيعًا فَيُنَبِّئُكُم بِمَا كُنتُمْ فِيهِ تَخْتَلِفُونَ

Al-Maidah 48

Say: Come I will recite what your Lord has forbidden to you—(remember) that you do not associate anything with Him and show kindness to your parents, and do not slay your children for (fear of) poverty—We provide for you and for them—and do not draw nigh to indecencies, those of them which are apparent and those which are concealed, and do not kill the soul which Allah has forbidden except for the requirements of justice; this He has enjoined you with that you may understand.

قُلْ تَعَالَوْا۟ أَتْلُ مَا حَرَّمَ رَبُّكُمْ عَلَيْكُمْ أَلَّا تُشْرِكُوا۟ بِهِۦ شَيْـًٔا وَبِٱلْوَٰلِدَيْنِ إِحْسَٰنًا وَلَا تَقْتُلُوٓا۟ أَوْلَٰدَكُم مِّنْ إِمْلَٰقٍ نَّحْنُ نَرْزُقُكُمْ وَإِيَّاهُمْ وَلَا تَقْرَبُوا۟ ٱلْفَوَٰحِشَ مَا ظَهَرَ مِنْهَا وَمَا بَطَنَ وَلَا تَقْتُلُوا۟ ٱلنَّفْسَ ٱلَّتِى حَرَّمَ ٱللَّهُ إِلَّا بِٱلْحَقِّ ذَٰلِكُمْ وَصَّىٰكُم بِهِۦ لَعَلَّكُمْ تَعْقِلُونَ

Al-Anam 151

And do not approach the property of the orphan except in the best manner until he attains his maturity; and give full measure and weight with justice—We do not impose on any soul a duty except to the extent of its ability; and when you speak, then be just though it be (against) a relative, and fulfill Allah's covenant; this He has enjoined you with that you may be mindful;

وَلَا تَقْرَبُوا۟ مَالَ ٱلْيَتِيمِ إِلَّا بِٱلَّتِى هِىَ أَحْسَنُ حَتَّىٰ يَبْلُغَ أَشُدَّهُۥ وَأَوْفُوا۟ ٱلْكَيْلَ وَٱلْمِيزَانَ بِٱلْقِسْطِ لَا نُكَلِّفُ نَفْسًا إِلَّا وُسْعَهَا وَإِذَا قُلْتُمْ فَٱعْدِلُوا۟ وَلَوْ كَانَ ذَا قُرْبَىٰ وَبِعَهْدِ ٱللَّهِ أَوْفُوا۟ ذَٰلِكُمْ وَصَّىٰكُم بِهِۦ لَعَلَّكُمْ تَذَكَّرُونَ

Al-Anam 152

The existence of these verses, quoted from the *Torah*, is a reason for the confirmation of the *Holy Torah* by Islam. At the time of the Prophet Moses thirteen scrolls of the *Holy Torah* were written, of which one was placed in the Holy Ark near the Holy Tables of the Decalogue, and the other twelve scrolls were granted to the twelve tribes so that they could make copies of them and take them with them at the time of their migration. In order that the *Holy Torah* may be read all over the world exactly at the same time, it has been divided according to the number of weeks in the year, and each part has been given a name. Thus each week the same specific part of the *Torah* is read out in synagogues everywhere.

Each word of the *Torah* must be pronounced correctly. This is the reason why no oral alteration has been possible. Every Jew, wherever he may be, is obliged to read the appropriate portion of the *Torah* each week.

CHAPTER ELEVEN

Misuse of the Religion

Those who use religion to deceive, hide the truth or profit from misrepresenting the true meaning of religion have done great damage to humanity over the course of history. People among the adherents of every religion with a heavenly book, have preyed on simple, illiterate, sincere and faithful believers and profited at their expense. Evidently the accounts of events rendered by such people differ from those of the true sages who preserved religion by their learning and sagacity.

In *Sura Al-Taubah 33* we read:

> He it is Who sent His Apostle with guidance and the religion of truth, that He might cause it to prevail over all religions, though the polytheists may be averse.

The actions of such deceivers in fact represent disobedience to the commands of the Almighty God, and their punishment is described here – in the *Sura Al-Hijir 33-35* we read:

> He said: I am not such that I should make obeisance to a mortal whom Thou hast created of the essence of black mud fashioned in shape.

> He said: Then get out of it, for surely you are driven away:

> And surely on you is curse until the day of judgment.

According to the views propounded in the *Gracious Koran* the doing of good deeds is not limited to merely praying. Belief in Almighty God, his messengers and angels and in the Day of Resurrection, helping the poor, keeping promises, being patient in times of poverty and hardship. All these are good deeds that are called for by the *Gracious Koran*.

The *Gracious Koran* compares those who read books without comprehending their contents to donkeys who carry numerous books on their backs. A parallel was drawn with those Jews who did not wish to learn the truth, who used to carry the *Holy Torah* with them without understanding its contents or putting its truth into practice.

> That is Allah's grace; He grants it to whom He pleases, and Allah is the Lord of mighty grace.

Sura Al-Jummah 4

Condemnation of Sinners in the *Gracious Koran*

The Almighty God expresses condemnation of Jewish sinners who befriended the atheists. He warns the believers who leave their faith and deny their religion, and emphasizes that the real believers in the Almighty God are not afraid of condemnations.

You will see many of them befriending those who disbelieve; certainly evil is that which their souls have sent before for them, that Allah became displeased with them and in chastisement shall they abide.

And had they believed in Allah and the prophet and what was revealed to him, they would not have taken them for friends, but most of them are transgressors.

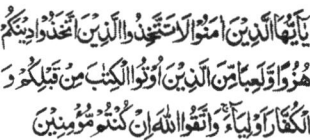

Al-Maidah 80-81

Shunning Those who Ridicule Religious Beliefs

Believers are recommended to shun those who ridicule religion, irrespective of the faith involved – *Al-Maidah 57*.

O you who believe! do not take for guardians those who take your religion for a mockery and a joke, from among those who were given the Book before you and the unbelievers; and be careful of (your duty to) Allah if you are believers.

The Testing of the Children of Israel

After some of the Children of Israel had strayed, Almighty God tested them – *Al-Maidah 71*. The Children of Israel promised not to repeat their errors and the Almighty God placed them high in his favour – but then they began to disobey again and were ungrateful. Thereupon the Almighty God withdrew his blessing and punished them as a lesson for future generations. These events are set forth in *Sura Al-Baqarah 63, 64,* and *66,* as follows:

And when we took a promise from you and lifted the mountain over you: Take hold of the law (Tavrat) We have given you with firmness and bear in mind what is in it, so that you may guard (against evil).

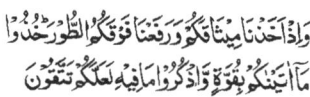

> Then you turned back after that; so were it not for the grace of Allah and His mercy on you, you would certainly have been among the losers.
>
> So We made them an example to those who witnessed it and those who came after it, and an admonition to those who guard (against evil).

After recalling the sins and deviations of Shanbeh's friends and their punishment, the Almighty God called upon the followers of the religions with a heavenly book to believe in what has been sent to them.

> O you who have been given the Book! believe that which We have revealed, verifying what you have, before We alter faces then turn them on their backs, or curse them as We cursed the violaters of the Sabbath, and the command of Allah shall be executed.

Al-Nisa 47

Dissenters Among the Followers of Religions with a Heavenly Book

The Almighty God tells His Prophet Mohammed that obviously those who did not believe Him are among those who did not believe His previous messengers either.

> But if they reject you, so indeed were rejected before you apostles who came with clear arguments and scriptures and the illuminating book.

Al-Imran 184

> O you who believe! do not take for intimate friends from among others than your own people; they do not fall short of inflicting loss upon you; they love what distresses you; vehement hatred has already appeared from out of their mouths, and what their breasts conceal is greater still; indeed, We have made the communications clear to you, if you will understand.

Al-Imran 118

In the next verses, Almighty God says that atheists and non-believers dislike the monotheists and believers, *Al-Imran 119*:

> Lo! you are they who will love them while they do not love you, and you believe in the Book (in) the whole of it; and when they meet you they say: We believe, and when they are alone, they bite the ends of their fingers in rage against you. Say: Die in your rage; surely Allah knows what is in the breasts.

Surely this refers to all atheists, because the monotheists had welcomed the expansion of Islam, which is also a monotheistic religion.

The Almighty God Tests Human Beings

The *Gracious Koran* mentions many cases in which the Almighty God has tested His slaves. The tests are usually related to life, which for humans is the dearest possession, their wealth and other worldly interests. Life is full of hardships and difficulties for those who want to adhere to their beliefs and maintain their religious and ethical values. It is a great achievement to pass such a Divine test.

> You shall certainly be tried respecting your wealth and your souls, and you shall certainly hear from those who have been given the Book before you and from those who are polytheists much annoying talk; and if you are patient and guard (against evil), surely this is one of the affairs (which should be) determined upon.

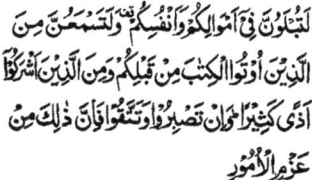

Al-Imran 186

Those Who Mislead Believers in Fact Mislead Themselves

The Almighty God considers those followers of a religion with a Holy Book who engage in misleading and condemning true believers.

> A party of the followers of the Book desire that they should lead you astray, and they lead not astray but themselves, and they do not perceive.

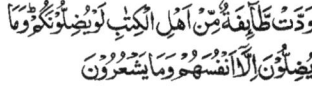

Al-Imran 69

Everyone is Responsible for his Own Deeds

In some sections of the *Gracious Koran* it states that each person will be judged according to his own deeds, and a person's sins will not be recorded against anybody else. Actually, nothing will change the judgment on the Day of Resurrection except good deeds and kindness. Recalling the blessings bestowed upon the Children of Israel, and appointing them to be the carriers of world civilization in the past, the Almighty God warns his slaves that every one will be judged according to their own deeds.

> O children of Israel, call to mind My favor which I bestowed on you and that I made you excel the nations.
>
> And be on your guard against a day when no soul shall avail another in the least neither shall any compensation be accepted from it, nor shall intercession profit it, nor shall they be helped.

Al-Baqarah 122-123

In the following verse, the Almighty God avers that the deeds and acts of nations and peoples will not form the basis for judgments of the successor and future generations, who will be not responsible for the deeds of their ancestors.

> This is a people that have passed away; they shall have what they earned and you shall have what you earn, and you shall not be called upon to answer for what they did.

Al-Baqarah 141

The Message and Command of the Almighty God in the *Holy Torah*

A group of Jewish residents of Medina had an audience with the Prophet Mohammed and asked him to adjudge between them, but at the same time they ignored the commands of the Almighty God. The Almighty God commanded His messenger not to be sad since honour was on His side.

> (They are) listeners of a lie, devourers of what is forbidden; therefore if they come to you, judge between them or turn aside from them, and if you turn aside from them, they shall not harm you in any way; and if you judge, judge between them with equity; surely Allah loves those who judge equitably.

Al-Maidah 42

Verses of Reprimand

And how do they make you a judge and they have the Tavrat wherein is Allah's judgment? Yet they turn back after that, and these are not the believers.

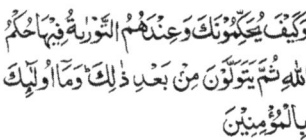

Al-Maidah 43

And let not their speech grieve you; surely might is wholly Allah's; He is the Hearing, the Knowing.

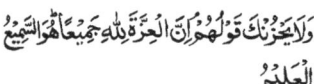

Yunis 65

Islam, the Religion of Obedience to the Commands of the Almighty God

After studying the verses which refer to the condemnation of sinners and emphasize that individuals, groups or nations, irrespective of their culture or civilization, are responsible for their own deeds, it is borne upon us that Islam is the religion of obedience – a Moslem is one who completely obeys the commands of Almighty God. The task of all the prophets has always been to call for obedience to the Almighty God and to prevent the worshipping of other gods.

And they say: Be Jews or Christians, you will be on the right course. Say: Nay! (we follow) the religion of Ibrahim, the Hanif, and he was not one of the polytheists.

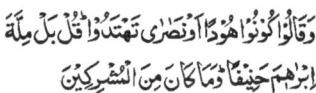

Al-Baqarah 135

Prophets are all equal and the Almighty God does not differentiate; all devoted themselves to guiding human beings and called for abstemiousness and adherence to monotheism, *Al-Baqarah 136*:

Say: We believe in Allah and (in) that which had been revealed to us, and (in) that which was revealed to Ibrahim and Ismail and Ishaq and Yaqoub and the tribes, and (in) that which was given to Musa and Isa, and (in) that which was given to the prophets from their Lord, we do not make any distinction between any of them, and to Him do we submit.

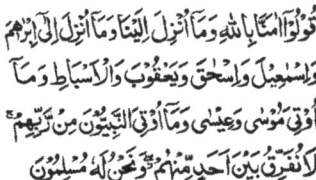

Friendship with the Followers of Other Religions with a Holy Book

Co-existence for Moslems and the followers of other religions with a heavenly book, based on mutual respect, as called for in the *Gracious Koran*, is the basis of Islamic international Law. Peace and co-existence should take the place of hostility and hatred. Following the holy commands of the Almighty God is the best recipe for creating mutual tolerance between followers of different religions. These are set forth in *Al-Muntahanah 7-8*.

It may be that Allah will bring about friendship between you and those whom you hold to be your enemies among them; and Allah is Powerful; and Allah is Forgiving, Merciful.	عَسَى اللّٰهُ أَنْ يَجْعَلَ بَيْنَكُمْ وَبَيْنَ الَّذِينَ عَادَيْتُمْ مِنْهُمْ مَوَدَّةً وَاللّٰهُ قَدِيرٌ وَاللّٰهُ غَفُورٌ رَحِيمٌ
Allah does not forbid you respecting those who have not made war against you on account of (your) religion, and have not driven you forth from your homes, that you show them kindness and deal with them justly; surely Allah loves the doers of justice.	لَا يَنْهَاكُمُ اللّٰهُ عَنِ الَّذِينَ لَمْ يُقَاتِلُوكُمْ فِي الدِّينِ وَلَمْ يُخْرِجُوكُمْ مِنْ دِيَارِكُمْ أَنْ تَبَرُّوهُمْ وَتُقْسِطُوا إِلَيْهِمْ إِنَّ اللّٰهَ يُحِبُّ الْمُقْسِطِينَ

Forgiveness and Ignorance

In general, forgiveness, ignorance and good deeds are recommended in all parts of the *Gracious Koran*, set forth in *Al-Shura 40-42*.

And the recompense of evil is punishment like it, but whoever forgives and amends, he shall have his reward from Allah; surely He does not love the unjust.	وَجَزَاءُ سَيِّئَةٍ سَيِّئَةٌ مِثْلُهَا فَمَنْ عَفَا وَأَصْلَحَ فَأَجْرُهُ عَلَى اللّٰهِ إِنَّهُ لَا يُحِبُّ الظَّالِمِينَ
And whoever defends himself after his being oppressed, these it is against whom there is no way (to blame).	وَلَمَنِ انْتَصَرَ بَعْدَ ظُلْمِهِ فَأُولَٰئِكَ مَا عَلَيْهِمْ مِنْ سَبِيلٍ
The way (to blame) is only against those who oppress men and revolt in the earth unjustly; these shall have a painful punishment.	إِنَّمَا السَّبِيلُ عَلَى الَّذِينَ يَظْلِمُونَ النَّاسَ وَيَبْغُونَ فِي الْأَرْضِ بِغَيْرِ الْحَقِّ أُولَٰئِكَ لَهُمْ عَذَابٌ أَلِيمٌ

Almighty God commands His messenger, who represents the personification of ethics, to react with goodness to evil, in order to create a strong bond with His followers.

Example and Teaching, Not Hostility and Hatred

My purpose in mentioning the verses of the *Gracious Koran* on the condemnation of sinners is merely to show the believers an example, not quarrel with them. In other words, the adventures of the Children of Israel and of those groups of Jews and the followers of other religions with a Holy Book who disobeyed the commands of the Almighty God and had to suffer the consequences should be regarded as an example not to be followed by the followers of religions with a heavenly book. In this way friendly co-existence among people of different cultures, especially the followers of religions with a heavenly book may be achieved.

Show Respect for, and Do Not Mock, the Ideas of Others

There are some ignorant, uncouth people who ridicule the ideas of others, and refuse to respect them. Evidently, friendship with such people, who humiliate others because of their ideas and beliefs, is not recommended and may even be harmful. As far as I know, Judaism and all other religions forbid such behaviour, which is both unwise and contemptible. Genuine and sincere friendship can only be based on respect for the other side's ideas. The *Gracious Koran* commands the Moslems and the believers to abstain from intimacy with those who mock and make sport of their faith. In *Sura Al-Maidah 57*:

O you who believe! do not take for guardians those who take your religion for a mockery and a joke, from among those who were given the Book before you and the unbelievers; and be careful of (your duty to) Allah if you are believers.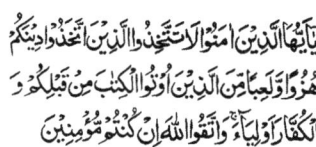

The Mercy and Grace of the Almighty God

Sura Al-Baqarah, of the *Gracious Koran* that was sent to the Prophet Mohammed, speaks of the Children of Israel who failed to keep their promises.

Then you turned back after that; so were it not for the grace of Allah and His mercy on you, you would certainly have been among the losers.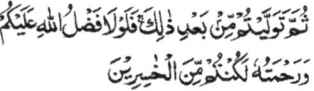

Sura Al-Baqarah 64

Despite this, the blessings of the Almighty God is applied to all His slaves, and His merciful rain washes the dust off sinners, making them clean, pure and restored.

Were All the Jews Sinners?

The *Gracious Koran* confirms that Moses was kind, merciful and of a generous disposition, and yet very powerful. He always enjoined his followers to do

CHAPTER ELEVEN

good deeds and be kind and merciful. As in other religions, there were among the Children of Israel some sinners and offenders, and they lived among the majority that were genuine and pure followers.

In *Sura Al-Baqarah 77-78*, the Almighty God reprimanded the sinners and enemies of human values, and points out what the terrible consequences of such behaviour will be. On the other hand, He has excluded the true and abstemious believers of the Jewish faith from His strictures. Divine justice does differentiate between sinners and pure slaves of the Almighty God. Regrettably, there are many sinners among the various nations and religions who violate the Divine commands and abjure moral principles. Indeed, sadly the number of such people is considerable. We may look at *Sura Al-Nisa 46*:

> Of those who are Jews (there are those who) alter words from their places and say: We have heard and we disobey and: Hear, may you not be made to hear! and: Raina, distorting (the word) with their tongues and taunting about religion; and if they had said (instead): We have heard and we obey, and hearken, and unzurna it would have been better for them and more upright; but Allah has cursed them on account of their unbelief, so they do not believe but a little.

مِنَ الَّذِينَ هَادُوا يُحَرِّفُونَ الْكَلِمَ عَن مَّوَاضِعِهِ وَيَقُولُونَ سَمِعْنَا وَعَصَيْنَا وَاسْمَعْ غَيْرَ مُسْمَعٍ وَرَاعِنَا لَيًّا بِأَلْسِنَتِهِمْ وَطَعْنًا فِي الدِّينِ وَلَوْ أَنَّهُمْ قَالُوا سَمِعْنَا وَأَطَعْنَا وَاسْمَعْ وَانظُرْنَا لَكَانَ خَيْرًا لَّهُمْ وَأَقْوَمَ وَلَٰكِن لَّعَنَهُمُ اللَّهُ بِكُفْرِهِمْ فَلَا يُؤْمِنُونَ إِلَّا قَلِيلًا

Obviously, those Jews who used to distort orally the words of the Almighty God were sinners and their account of events differs from that of the God-fearing, abstemious real believers. It is neither appropriate nor just to draw inferences regarding a whole group of people, a nation, or believers in a religion, most of whom are honest and pure, from the behaviour of a few. I believe that everyone should contribute his share to the removal of obstacles from the way to peace, understanding and co-existence among the followers of the Ibrahimian religions.

According to the *Gracious Koran*, Moslems are commanded to make peace with the followers of religions with a Holy Book if the latter propose this and trust in the Almighty God. In *Sura Al-Anfal 61*:

> And if they incline to peace, then incline to it and trust in Allah; surely He is the Hearing, the Knowing.

وَإِن جَنَحُوا لِلسَّلْمِ فَاجْنَحْ لَهَا وَتَوَكَّلْ عَلَى اللَّهِ إِنَّهُ هُوَ السَّمِيعُ الْعَلِيمُ

Equally, the *Gracious Koran* commands Moslems to fight against those who begin wars against their religion, their lives and their honour.

> What is the matter with you, then, that you have become two parties about the

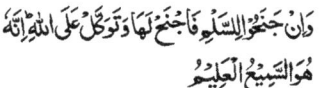

(continued next page)

hypocrites, while Allah has made them return (to unbelief) for what they have earned? Do you wish to guide him whom Allah has caused to err? And whomsoever Allah causes to err, you shall by no means find a way for him.

Sura Al-Nisa 88

They desire that you should disbelieve as they have disbelieved, so that you might be (all) alike; therefore take not from among them friends until they fly (their homes) in Allah's way; but if they turn back, then seize them and kill them wherever you find them, and take not from among them a friend or a helper.

Sura Al-Nisa 89

Except those who reach a people between whom and you there is an alliance, or who come to you, their hearts shrinking from fighting you or fighting their own people; and if Allah had pleased, He would have given them power over you, so that they should have certainly fought you; therefore if they withdraw from you and do not fight you and offer you peace, then Allah has not given you a way against them.

Sura Al-Nisa 90

The road to peace, understanding and cooperation can best and most safely be paved by negotiation. In this process scientists and intellectuals have a great role to play. By including passages concerning the need for friendship and understanding with religious minorities in schoolbooks and other educational material, I hope to inculcate in children a sense of kindness and tolerance, instead of encouraging them to indulge in hatred and hostility, as happened so often in the past.

The verses of the *Gracious Koran* were sent during the twenty-three years of Mohammed's activity as a prophet. Each one was sent for a particular occasion or situation, and was addressed to specific persons or peoples. It is therefore quite wrong to blame all the Children of Israel at all times in history and wherever they may be at any given moment for the sins some Jews committed in the small city of Medina (Yasreb) 1,400 years ago, at the time of the Prophet Mohammed, when they attracted punishment because they had conspired with polytheists!

All the *Suras* of the *Gracious Koran* begin with the words: 'In the name of God, the compassionate and the merciful', and these words must surely be given some meaning.

The interpreters of the *Gracious Koran* opine that the above sentence that opens the *Koran*'s *Suras* is, in fact, an independent verse. The Almighty God always commands us to be just and practice forgiveness and generosity. The purpose of religion is to bring about the salvation of human beings in the two worlds on the basis of justice, honesty and kindness. Religion causes people to be orderly, ethical and observant of the law. There are many cases in history that show how, through religion, peoples became less ferocious and aggressive and began to behave justly, bravely and in a civilized manner.

The three Ibrahimian religions hold in common the belief that the Almighty God is just and unique, that He was the sole creator of the world and of life on it, and that He is the source of all goodness in the world.

These three great religions believe that the Almighty God wants human beings to be peaceful, to lead lives of grace and to be just. They are also united in the belief that man is unable to fathom the essence of God.

Verses of Reprimand

Islam permits comment and interpretation. I therefore I feel it necessary to explain the meaning of *Sura Al-Baqarah 61*: one of the Verses of Reprimand. According to this verse the Children of Israel aroused the anger of the Almighty God, and were reprimanded and condemned by Him, because they were stubborn and disobedient. We know that the threatened punishment was actually meted out, and this fact attests to the miraculous nature of the *Gracious Koran*: the mentioned verse was sent to the Prophet Mohammed in the Hijaz, where today there is not a single Jew present. The Jews who used to live in the cities and village of that area, who were the ones referred to in *Sura Al-Baqarah 141*, have become extinct. They were punished for their deeds, and no one can blame the Jews living at present for those deeds.

1. Holding the deeds of a group of Jewish sinners who lived 1,400 year ago against all the Children of Israel is against the justice of the Almighty God, that justice in which we all believe and which is also mentioned in the *Gracious Koran*.

2. Various verses of the *Gracious Koran* promise safety and deliverance to the followers of the religions with a heavenly book.

3. In the countries that are in the neighboring region of the Hijaz, such as Egypt, Sudan, Yemen, Syria and Lebanon, Jews, Christians and Moslems have been living together.

4. Although there have been contemptible persons among the Jews – as there are in any nation – there have also been honourable ones among them. They have occupied high positions, such as prime minister or other elevated governmental positions, in America, Europe and elsewhere, including in Moslem countries. Jews have

been notable in areas of science and some have received Nobel Peace Prizes for their contributions to humanity.

5. Since the beginning of Islam, the Jews have lived in peace and prosperity in Moslem countries when those were ruled by pious rulers, and they lived miserably when cruel rulers were in power.

6. The verses of the *Gracious Koran* do not make exceptions; the Jews are not all poor or wealthy.

Ozair is mentioned in the *Sura Al-Taubah 29-30*; the Children of Israel did not have any relations with the Munafiqun, because they are monotheists and believe in the unique God, his Prophets, and the Day of Judgment, and they consider unlawful what the Almighty God and his prophets have forbidden. Since Moses and Jesus were prophets, their orders are as effective as the commands of the Almighty God and must be obeyed without any excuse.

At the time of the Prophet Mohammed there were some tribes that pretended to be monotheists but were in fact not true converts, and they caused great distress to the Prophet Mohammed. We see that these two verses of *Sura Al-Taubah* have been repeated; this demonstrates that the Munafiqun only pretended to be Moslems, but actually did not believe in Islam. They in fact constituted the reason why so many verses were sent in *Sura Al-Taubah* and the cause for the sending of the whole *Sura* is to be found in the struggle against the Munafiqun.

In the *Sura Al-Baqarah* it is confirmed that all the prophets are equal and the Almighty God does not differentiate between them. The task of all of them is to lead man to monotheism, justice and good deeds. Of course each nation contained sinners and persons who disobeyed the Holy commands. Among the terrible and unforgettable events in human history, we find the killing of Imam Ali while he was at prayer, and the murder of the grandchildren of the Prophet Mohammed by a Moslem. My purpose in mentioning these crimes is to show that there were sinners also among the Moslems.

Chapter Twelve

•

Prophet of Islam and Possession of a Heavenly Book

The Situation of Iran at the Time of the Advent of Islam

We will now consider the behaviour of the Gracious Prophet of Islam towards the followers of religions with a Holy Book, especially the Jews, and mention the relevant verses of the *Gracious Koran*. I will also make reference to some points of the philosophy by virtue of which Mohammed was anointed as Prophet, and at the end we will deal with the manner in which the Prophet Mohammed behaved towards the followers of religions with a heavenly book, in compliance with the commands of the *Gracious Koran*.

A brief examination of the condition of Arabia before Islam, of the lives of the Arabs and the social conditions in Iran at the time of the Sassanids, will help us obtain a better understanding of our subject:

Mission of Prophet Mohammed – 610-632
(Gregorian Calendar)

Iran and Byzantium were two great empires at the time of Yazdegerd the Third. In Iran, the Zoroastrian religious leaders conceived their religion as being the basis of the dignity of their country, and insisted that all citizens take an interest in the religion. Non-Zoroastrians were persecuted and prejudices against them were fostered. Internal tensions in Iran, and especially at the court, were at their peak. Murder and assassination were common, and even touched some of the princes of the Iran Royal family. This situation had prevailed since the times of Firuz. The Christians and Jews then living in Iran felt so insecure that they gradually left the country. Zoroastrianism, the formal state religion at the time of the Sassanids, was changing, becoming more superficial and empty of real content. Decay and decline were fast approaching the Iranian Empire.

At this time, Christianity, whose founder had been a symbol of kindness and humaneness, and who had at his time attempted to defend the Jews in Jerusalem against the oppressions of the Romans, itself became a weapon in the hands of the Romans at a later stage in history. The Romans, who had killed the Prophet Jesus, became the leaders of Christianity, but they were bereft of the kindness and humaneness, which were supposed to be part of the religion. They acted without mercy to remove any obstacles which stood in their way, and Nero and Caligula were typical of the kind of ruler who headed

Rome at the time. Amongst other misdeeds, the Jews living in Rome were annihilated, ultimately.

Iran and Byzantium, the two eastern empires, had been weakened by lengthy wars in which they had been involved with each other. The time was ripe for new thought and the development of new civilizations.

Yazdegerd III became king of Iran in 634 C.E., during the second year after the death of the Prophet Mohammed, who died in 632 C.E. Important events happened in Arabia during the years from 610 C.E., when Mohammed was anointed as the Prophet, until his death, especially after the Hejira (622 C.E.) to Yasreb (Medina). In order to know how that period affected Iran and its Jewish population we must examine some events that took place earlier:

Before the advent of the Prophet Mohammed, the Children of Ishmael had forgotten the monotheism of their ancestor, the Prophet Abraham (The Prophet Mohammed was a resident of Hijaz and the offspring of Ishmael – son of the Prophet Abraham). Prior to Mohammed being anointed as a prophet there had been three hundred and sixty idols, which represented all the Goddesses and Gods, worshipped by the Arabs. Offerings of human sacrifices were usual and customary at that time.

The people of Arabia were divided into two groups: The Hazaree, who used to live in the cities and villages, and the Badawi, who were nomads and lived in tents. As a result of social contacts with the Jews, some Arabs gradually became familiar with the Jewish religion, and were willing to convert to Judaism. This conversion was easy because they had already been circumcised. Usually, when the leader of a tribe decided to convert to some religion, all his followers would do the same. Bani Kananeh of the Ghoraysh family, and some tribes of Oss and Khazarge did, in fact, convert to Judaism.

In the year 500 according to the Gregorian calendar, Abu Gharibeh, the king of Yemen, being on his way to a war with Ghobad, surrounded the city of Yasreb (Medina) in which many Jews were living. As some of the inhabitants of that city had killed his son, it was known that Abu Gharibeh was intent on taking revenge on the population. Two Jewish sages, Kaab and Assad, were chosen to ask his forgiveness. During their meeting with the king they succeeded in telling him the essence of the Jewish religion, and finally he and his army converted.

During the reign of Zonovas, the grandson of Abu Gharibeh, all the citizens of Yemen converted to Judaism in the year 520. Zonovas governed for ten years and was finally defeated by a king of the Christians, whose object was to remove the Jews because they did not permit Christians to trade freely in their country. The defeated Zonovas was not able to escape and threw himself into the sea. Thereafter, the city of Yemen was sacked and its inhabitants were slaughtered. As a result, the influence of the Jews in Arabia diminished. Following this event, the residents of Yasreb (Medina) who were concerned that the Jewish population of their town might increase, rose up against the local Jews and killed their leaders.

Chapter Twelve

In the 6th century the Jews regained their power and influence. According to Georgi Zeidan: 'The Arabs of the Hijaz had lived primitive lives, devoid of culture and not touched by any civilization. The arrival of Jews in the Hijaz following upon the oppression of the Romans, since the time of the Prophet Moses, and especially after the destruction of Jerusalem, changed their situation.

'Some Egyptians also emigrated to Mecca and Medina. Most of the Jews preferred to move to Medina because their fellow believers, the Oss and Khazarge tribes, were living there. Immigration of Jews to the Hijaz greatly influenced the social conditions of the Arabs. The Hajj ceremony, offering of sacrifices, marriage and divorce, ceremonial feasts and the election of priests were customs that the Hijaz Arabs learnt from the newly immigrated Jews. Stories from the *Torah* and the *Talmud* were also made available and became familiar to the Arabs of the Hijaz.'

According to Georgi Zeidan, the Moslems spread the religion of Islam among the people of Medina. It could be said that the Jews were among the factors instrumental in spreading Islam in Medina, since, in contrast to the atheists in Mecca, they were monotheists and followers of a religion with a heavenly book. Moreover, they knew the meaning of heavenly inspiration and believed in the missions of the prophets. Also, they were aware of the fact that the spread of Islam would not interfere with their business activities, whereas the people of Mecca believed that the spreading of Islam would limit the attention paid to the idols in their city, and as a consequence commerce in their city would suffer. The Jews, in common with the other inhabitants of Medina, welcomed the spread of the new religion, and hoped to attract the Prophet Mohammed to come to their city.

Georgi Zeidan adds the following:

The Romans may have differed on many things, but they were united and in full agreement with each other on one subject, to wit, the persecution and torture of the Jews. This situation bothered the Jews to such an extent that, although they were somewhat avaricious, they helped the Moslems financially as much as possible in order to take revenge on the Romans. Financial assistance was not the only kind of help the Jews extended to the Moslems in the latter's confrontation with the Romans. As an example we can cite the instance when Moslem soldiers had laid siege to the city of Gheysarieh (Caesarea) for seven years, but had not been able to capture it because every night about 100,000 soldiers used to guard the towers and walls of the city. Moavieh, the commander of the Moslem forces, asked the Jews to help him. A Jew called Youssef lead the Moslems into the city through the water canal system. All he asked for was protection for himself and his family. The conquest of Gheysarieh was thus achieved purely because of the help provided by the Jew Youssef.

In another case, Abu Obideh, the commander of a Moslem armed force concluded a peace agreement with the people of Samaria, who were all Jewish. He exempted them from having to pay tribute provided they were ready to help the Moslems.

History shows that at the time of Roman oppression, especially during the first century C.E., (at the time of the destruction of the second Temple in Jerusalem, the defeat of Bar Kochba, and even at the time of the persecution of the Jews by Artaxerxes, Sassanid, Firooz and Hormoz) some Iranian Jews emigrated to Arabia, which was apparently a safer place. It was also rumoured that Joshua ben Nun sent some Jews to fight the Amalekites, and they resided in Yasreb and Kheybar. Furthermore, it also appears that at the time of Saul and David some Jews had settled in the Hijaz. There is also anecdotal evidence that at the time of Solomon, who used to send his ships to Ofir, that the Jews had established a business branch in Southern Arabia for the administration of business with India.

It has also been related that that some Jews had gone to the Hijaz as refugees at the time of the destruction of the First Temple by Nebuchadnezzar. At that time the situation of the Jews in Judea and Europe was very bad, whereas in Arabia and Hijaz they were free, safe, and equal to the Arabs. The Arabs who were converted to Judaism were very familiar with the techniques of war and were able to fight skillfully and bravely.

The Jews often had agreements with the Arab tribes, and used to enter wars on their side as they had undertaken to do. They were also skilled in agriculture and most of the time helped the Arabs. The history of the Jews in Arabia during the first century before the advent of Islam was really brilliant. Briefly, there were three Jewish tribes in Arabia in addition to the one in the North. Yasreb (Medina) was the centre for all the Jewish tribes. There were some Jews in the north of Medina who lived like nomadic tribes. Some Jews also used to live in Medina where the temple of the idols was located. There were many Jews living in Yemen as well.

There were some characteristics common to both Jews and Arabs, such as language, customs, exclusiveness of race, ways of living, hospitality, and revengefulness. The Jews who lived in the south engaged in trade, whereas those living in the north lived as nomads. Since the Jews were interested in poetry and literature, were familiar with their history and religion, and above all were monotheists and literate, they were called Men of Books, to distinguish them from the Arabs.

The Arabian Jews fully accepted and respected the *Talmud* and lived according to its precepts. They were in touch with their spiritual centre in Tiberias. They regarded Jerusalem as their Temple. The city of Yasreb (Medina) was the centre of Jewish studies in the Hijaz. The relations between Arabs and Jews were friendly and peaceful. The ancestors of both Yaghtani and Ishmaeli Arabs had been Jews (on their fathers' side).

As a consequence of the points mentioned at the beginning of this chapter and the unstable conditions prevailing in Iran and Byzantium, Arabia was not stable either. Although the Jews were monotheists and some Arabs had converted to Judaism, the tradition of idol worshipping continued to prevail in most of Arabia. The practice of burying daughters alive was still prevalent among the inhabitants. In fact, these aspects represented a serious threat for the monotheistic Jews.

At this phase, the people of Arabia were divided into three categories:

1. Idol worshippers, who were in the majority.

2. Children of Israel, who were men of books and not of war, and were in the minority.

3. People who had originally been Arabs and had converted to Judaism and remained addicted to advocating war.

In this state of affairs, the large country of Arabia was in need of a great religious leader; a Prophet who would be able to lead the population and help them forget the unworthy traditions and habits that had become entwined with their religious and national principles. And again, one of the children of Abraham was chosen for this great mission that also involved a cultural revolution.

Some writers may, for different reasons, have shown the Jews as being opposed to this revolution. Some others have indulged in generalizations and ascribed to all Children of Israel involvement in some local trivial individual or social events that occurred owing to the existence of tribal clashes between idol worshippers (first category) and Arab converts to Judaism (third category).

The Children of Israel in fact welcomed the advent of Islam, which would disseminate monotheism among the ignorant and idol worshippers of Arabia. They preferred to live in an environment of monotheistic faith and justice. The trivial and isolated events that arose as a result of the intrigues of the non-Jewish Abdullah Ibn Abi should not be described as involving all Jews, and the statements of some self-styled Moslem Mullahs should be ignored.

The Jews, especially those who lived in Arabia and Asia Minor, were very glad about the appearance of a religion similar to their own that was also based on monotheistic principles. They observed that idol worshipping and ignorance were being curtailed. Moreover, the oppression exercised by the Eastern Roman Empire, which had converted to 'Christianity' (not exactly according to the precepts of Jesus) had caused them great concern, and consequently the coming of Islam was a heavenly gift for them. That is the reason for the serious endeavors of the Jews to help the promulgation of Islam. Abdollah Ibn Salam, and many other inhabitants of Medina, were examples of people who engaged in this activity. Later, the Jews played a significant role in the victories of Islam in North Africa and Spain. They knew that their freedom, peace and security would depend on Islam being successful.

At the beginning, the city of Mecca, which was the centre for idol worship, did not welcome the Prophet. He was forced to leave, but was then warmly welcomed at Medina, a town that contained a high concentration of Jews and where also non-Jews were broadly familiar with the Jewish beliefs. Here, discussing monotheism and religions based on the unity of God was not considered a strange subject and indeed occupied the minds of many people. Many inhabitants converted to Islam and it was here that the basis of the success of Islam and its ultimate victory was laid. The Prophet Mohammed died in 632 C.E. He bequeathed to his followers laws based on justice and equality, as well as rules for behaviour in an orderly society. None of his rules prescribed any limits for the Children of Israel or the Jewish nation.

Characteristics of Arabs Before Islam

Seven particular characteristics are mentioned concerning the ignorance of the Arabs before Islam. Some of these characteristics do in fact persist up to this day.

1. Ignorant Arabs were not orderly and obedient.

2. They were self-reliant and committed to their tribes.

3. Racism and extreme nationalism were (and still are) part of their make-up. In the pre-Islam era killing, plunder, raping, lying, and betrayal were considered justified as means for reaching their nationalistic goals. (By the mercy of the Prophet Mohammed and the teachings of the *Gracious Koran* these activities are now forbidden).

4. Most Arabs were hospitable, a characteristic also known to exist among Moslems.

5. Arabs used to be content in their lives, a matter difficult to understand for an outsider.

6. The Arabs were physically strong with slim bodies. They were diligent and warlike.

7. Arabs had chosen the camel as their companion, told many fables about this animal and referred to it by many names.

CHAPTER TWELVE

A Brief Look at the Prophetic Mission of the Prophet Mohammed

I find it opportune to quote an article written by the learned Mohammed Reza Hakimi, published in the *Etelaat* newspaper. From it we can glean some details regarding the social conditions prevailing at the time of the appearance of Islam and the mission of the Prophet Mohammed: 'The dry land of Arabia, straddling the route between Asia and Europe, was an important centre of commerce. Indian and Chinese goods were transported to Egypt and the West via Arabia. In ancient Europe Indian products (precious stones, perfumes and rare animals) arriving by way of the trade route passing through Arabia, were mistakenly considered as being of Arabian origin'.

There were in fact some materials originating in the southern parts of Arabia, such as odorous gums, myrrh and frankincense, that were used in European temples. At the time of the prophetic mission only about one sixth of the population of Arabia were city dwellers; the others were nomads (tent dwellers) or desert dwellers. Some of them habitually killed and plundered. Camels and swords were their best friends.

One of the poets of the Era of Ignorance says: 'We usually plunder and assault our neighbours. Sometimes, if we cannot find anybody, we plunder our brothers!'

These reprehensible deeds were abolished by the appearance of Islam. The primitive Arabs, fiercely independent and obstinate in their ways, preferred living the hard life of the desert. They were brave and hospitable, and at the same time reckless in plundering and pillaging as part of their daily live. Arabs living in the city, on the other hand, engaged in trade, or breeding animals. At that time, before the advent of Islam, each tribe was independent, and the other tribes were considered to be strangers. Killing was a normal thing for them, irrespective of whether they lived in towns or in the desert. When Shanfari, a poet who lived in the Era of Ignorance, was insulted he killed ninety-nine people. Besous, a woman living at that time, had a camel called Mirage. Once when the camel entered the lands belonging to Colaib the latter shot at it. Jessas, a nephew of Besous, killed Colaib. This simple incident caused a war of forty years duration between the tribes of Bakr and Salaab.

The House of Kabba was the most important source of income for some members of the Ghoraysh tribe. All tribes because of its history respected this house and also because of the fact that it housed 300 to 600 idols, each of which belonged to a tribe.

The above provided a brief look at the cultural, ethical and economical aspects of a people living in the birthplace of a Prophetic mission. The situation in other countries was not much better. Even well known countries were embroiled with their own problems. In Iran, different religions existed side by side causing friction and disturbing the peace of mind of the population. Rulers customarily meted out death to their subjects with impunity.

When the year of the prophetic mission arrived, Mohammed climbed up the

Hara Mountain. There, at the time of his designation as a prophet, the Archangel Gabriel came to him. Mohammed narrates: 'I was asleep when Gabriel came to me and said: "Read!" I said: "I don't know how to read." He held me strongly and then released me. He said again: "Read." I said: "What should I read?" He said: "Read in the name of your God who created."

'I came out of the cave and as I was making my way on the mountain I heard a voice call from the sky, saying: "Oh Mohammed! You are the Prophet of God and I am Gabriel". I looked at the sky and saw Gabriel as the figure of a man on the horizon. He said: "Oh Mohammed! You are the Prophet of God and I am Gabriel." I stopped and kept looking at him. I neither went forward nor backward. I did not look sideways, but continued to see him.' Thus Mohammed was appointed as a prophet when he was forty years old, and he was sent out to humanity to create the greatest revolution in the history of mankind.

When Mohammed came back from Mount Hara and announced his prophetic mission, his wife Khadijeh and his cousin Ali Ibn Abitaleb believed in him, and converted to Islam. For three years Mohammed's ordination was kept a secret, and only thereafter he acted explicitly, calling people to adhere to monotheism and be saved with the dictum: 'Say there is no God but Allah.'

In this way the Prophet Mohammed continued to spread the faith. His faithful followers, whom he educated, continued to disseminate Islam in order to improve society and make it safe and true.

The Prophet Mohammed suffered greatly in the course of his mission. He said: 'No prophet has ever suffered as much as I have.' The Moslem religion was spread in nearly all parts of Arabia at the time of the Prophet Mohammed. Later, the faithful Moslem believers disseminated this religion in other parts of the world including in Iran.

The *Gracious Koran* from the Moslem Point of View

In the eyes of the Moslems the *Gracious Koran* is the only heavenly book that has not been changed. The *Koran* calls upon human beings at all times to do correct deeds, to practice justice and sincerity, kindness, patience, honour, and to engage in scholarly occupations. The collection of the verses of the *Gracious Koran* occurred at the time of the Third Caliph Uthman.

This was a brief look at the prophetic mission of Mohammed, a mission that caused enormous change and created a basis for one of the great eternal religions and civilizations. Historians and sociologists all over the world are unanimous in acknowledging its impact and dignity.

Other Views About the Prophetic Mission

All researchers, whether they be Moslems or not, are agreed that Mohammed's Prophetic Mission represented a spiritual and moral revolution whose impact is felt undiminished today, although it happened fifteen centuries ago. The following is a précis of an article that looks at the Prophetic Mission from another angle:

> The Prophetic Mission can be regarded from different points of view: Under one aspect it is an exceptional phenomenon, and on the other hand its subject matters are popular and universal aspects of life. The physically perceived divine inspiration, the special relationship with the Almighty God, and the particular spiritual personality of the Prophet Mohammed can be classified as being in the first category, while the social and individual aspects of the mission would place it in the second category.
>
> As an individual and a member of society each one of us bears responsibilities for his family, society, school, neighbourhood, city, region, country and the world; and this implies readiness to show sympathy, and to help people who suffer pain and misery.
>
> The most serious threat to humanity at present is the excessive attachment to material things, which is evident everywhere from the individual to governments. It is thus not to be wondered at that thoughtful and moderate people in the East and West are groping for new ideals that may enable them to reach a 'spiritual civilization'.

Gracious Koran

There are many books about the Prophet Mohammed, but too little has been written about the religions with a heavenly book. Mohammed was designated as a prophet at the age of forty. Before that he was living in Mecca and Medina and was known as an honest and trustworthy man. These characteristics caused people to help him. At the age of forty he experienced the Divine direction and was named a prophet in order to guide and save the atheists from ignorance, idolatry, polytheism and corruption, and lead them to monotheism, knowledge and deliverance.

The *Gracious Koran* Speaks to Us

The *Gracious Koran* is the best source for understanding the prophetic mission. Hereunder I paraphrase some of its verses that are relevant to this matter:

He it is Who raised among the illiterates an Apostle from among them-	هُوَٱلَّذِى بَعَثَ فِى ٱلْأُمِّيِّـۧنَ رَسُولًا مِّنْهُمْ يَتْلُوا۟

(continued next page)

selves, who recites to them His communications and purifies them, and teaches them the Book and the Wisdom, although they were before certainly in clear error,

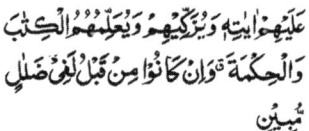

Al Jumuah 2

Almighty God has, in fact, conferred a great benefit on human beings by leading them to faith and deliverance, assigning prophets from among themselves, their own society and language, to guide them.

Certainly Allah conferred a benefit pon the believers when He raised among hem an Apostle from among themselves, eciting to them His communications and urifying them, and teaching them the ook and the wisdom, although before hat they were surely in manifest error.

Al-Imran 164

The following verses, *Al-Anam 155-157,* contain answers to the criticisms of some atheists:

And this is a Book We have revealed, blessed; therefore follow it and guard (against evil) that mercy may be shown to you.

Lest you say that the Book was only revealed to two parties before us and We were truly unaware of what they read.

Or (lest you should say: If the Book had been revealed to us, we would certainly have been better guided than they; so indeed there has come to you clear proof from your Lord, and guidance and mercy. Who then is more unjust than he who rejects Allah's communications and turns away from them? We will reward those who turn away from Our communications with an evil chastisement because they turned away.

The reference to 'prophets who speak the language of the people' does not merely mean to be able to speak Arabic in Arab lands, or to speak Hebrew to people using that language; the main implied idea is that the prophet is of the same background, steeped in the problems, customs, traditions, mysteries and secrets of his people. He is not a stranger to the people, who has arrived from an imaginary or idealized heaven. The social and individual aspects of the mission are the second point of view.

CHAPTER TWELVE

> And We did not send any apostle but with the language of his people, so that he might explain to them clearly; then Allah makes whom He pleases err and He guides whom He pleases, and He is the Mighty, the Wise.
>
> And certainly We sent Musa with Our communications, saying: Bring forth your people from utter darkness into light and remind them of the days of Allah; most surely there are signs in this for every patient, grateful one.

Ibrahim 4-5

As the *Gracious Koran* is not opposed to other religions that have a heavenly book, the fight of the followers of such religions against Islam is unwise and unfair. In fact, it is against their own religious principles, which strictly recommend peace.

> And We have revealed to you the Book with the truth, verifying what is before it of the Book and a guardian over it, therefore judge between them by what Allah has revealed, and do not follow their low desires (to turn away) from the truth that has come to you; for every one of you did We appoint a law and a way, and if Allah had pleased He would have made you (all) a single people, but that He might try you in what He gave you, therefore strive with one another to hasten to virtuous deeds; to Allah is your return, of all (of you), so He will let you know that in which you differed;

Al-Maidah 48

I wish this verse would be inscribed on everybody's doorjamb, as is the custom of the Children of Israel who inscribe there a prayer so that they should not forget the holiness of the Almighty God in order to remind human beings that they should be saintly, pure and aware of the goodness of their religion.

This Holy verse confirms the Holy Bible – the Almighty God has given to each of us a law, a way and pattern of life, and if He had wished to do so He surely could have made us one people professing one faith.

Calling the Followers of Religions with a Heavenly Book

By studying the *Gracious Koran*, which in fact is the constitutional law of Moslems, we will learn what the Prophet Mohammed expected from the followers of a religion with a heavenly book, and in the same way, what these followers expected and understood from Islam and its prophet. The first lesson that the *Gracious Koran* teaches us is that faith and belief cannot be acquired by force or pressure, and these should not be used in making people accept ideas and beliefs.

> There is no compulsion in religion; truly the right way has become clearly distinct from error; therefore, whoever disbelieves in the Shaitan and believes in Allah, he indeed has laid hold on the firmest handle, which shall not break off, and Allah is Hearing, Knowing.

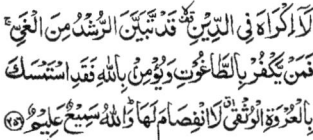

Al-Baqarah 256

Jews and Christians have their own holy books, parallel to the *Gracious Koran*. The prophets of all religions have the same message – to wit, exhortations to be monotheists, and to abstain from sins, crimes and corruption. According to the prophets, by worshipping the Almighty God one can retain divine, ethical values and be saved in the two worlds. In these matters the Almighty God has made no distinction between his prophets.

Let us look at *Sura Al-Baqarah 136*:

> Say: We believe in Allah and (in) that which had been revealed to us, and (in) that which was revealed to Ibrahim and Ismail and Ishaq and Yaqoub and the tribes, and (in) that which was given to Musa and Isa, and (in) that which was given to the prophets from their Lord, we do not make any distinction between any of them, and to Him do we submit.

Prophets are sent for the purpose of arousing hope and fear; they address all peoples irrespective of their language, race, colour or gender, and whether they are poor or rich. Only good deeds can confer advantages to one person over another.

> And We send not messengers but as announcers of good news and givers of warning; then whoever believes and acts aright, they shall have no fear, nor shall they grieve.

Al-Anam 48

> And if your Lord had pleased He would certainly have made people a single nation, and they shall continue to differ.

Hud 118

Peoples and nations each have their own way of life and system of community. It is the task of the prophets to urge them towards the Almighty God, which is in fact the only true direction.

CHAPTER TWELVE

> To every nation We appointed acts of devotion which they observe, therefore they should not dispute with you about the matter and call to your Lord; most surely you are on a right way.
>
> *Al-Haj 67*

Needless to say, people are not equal; education, their manner of speaking and behaviour does differ. Everywhere there are two-faced, insincere people, offenders and sinners, and they must be regarded entirely separately from true and honest people who pray to the Almighty God regularly, help others, do good deeds, and prefer spirituality to materialism.

We have already mentioned the *Sura Al-Imran 113-115* in which the Almighty God promised great rewards and happiness to people who are true followers of the religions with a heavenly book, and believe in Him and the Day of Judgment; those who pray regularly, abstain from doing what is unlawful and do what is good and lawful.

The polytheism of Arabs is skilfully described in *Sura Fatir 42*:

> And they swore by Allah with the strongest of their oaths that if there came to them a warner they would be better guided than any of the nations; but when there came to them a warner it increased them in naught but aversion,

Correct Appreciation of the *Gracious Koran*'s Verses

When surveying the verses from the *Gracious Koran* referred to in this and preceding chapters, it can be seen that the Prophet Mohammed had a peaceful relationship with the followers of other religions with a heavenly book. He never fought them, but tried to communicate with them kindly and logically. He used anger and roughness merely as a last resort in order to carry out his duties as guide and advisor.

The Prophet Mohammed and the Children of Israel

The Prophet Mohammed concluded an interesting and singular agreement with the Jews before he left Mecca for Medina. The contents of the agreement is as follows: This is the agreement between the Prophet Mohammed, the messenger of God, and the Jews. The believers are to know that Moslems are one nation and should behave like a single body. They should conclude agreements with the Jews that are similar to this agreement.

1. In peacetime Jews and Moslems will have equal rights.

2. In case of necessity Moslems will help and support Jews.

3. The Jews and the residents of Medina (Yasreb) are considered as one nation.

4. Moslems will treat Jews kindly and in a friendly manner.

5. Jews will be as free to perform their religious duties as Moslems are.

6. The tribes that are allied with the Jews will be supported by Moslems.

7. If a Jew is oppressed by others, the Moslems will pursue and punish them.

8. Both sides will respect each other's friends, and Jews will help Moslems in guarding Medina and it suburbs.

9. In case of disputes arising between Jews and Moslems, the Prophet Mohammed will adjudge them according to the laws of the *Gracious Koran* and the *Holy Torah*.

10. This agreement was concluded between Jews and Moslems.

This agreement was soon signed and accepted by all the Jewish tribes living in Medina and its suburbs, such as Bani Nazir, Bani Gharizeh, Bani Ghingha.

The Children of Israel and Mohammed's Prophetic Mission

Various verses in the *Gracious Koran* (Compassionate Verses) clearly indicate that the Prophet Mohammed recognized the religions that have a heavenly book and had agreed to their being at liberty to pursue their religious duties. (See Chapter Six on Confirmation of the *Holy Torah*).

The opinion and assessment of the Children of Israel regarding the mission of the Prophet Mohammed is clear. The Jews of Mecca and Medina welcomed him because he advocated monotheism, and called upon the idol worshippers to abandon their ignorance. The *Sura Yunis 47*, which we have already mentioned, is a good proof of the aforesaid (see also *Sura Al Jummah 2* pp 89-90).

And every nation had an apostle; so when their apostle came, the matter was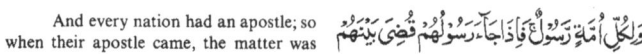

(continued next page)

CHAPTER TWELVE

decided between them with justice and they shall not be dealt with unjustly.

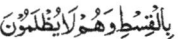

The Prophet Mohammed explicitly introduces himself as a prophet who leads and guides the atheists and idol worshippers to monotheism. The Jews did not put the well being of the Moslems in Medina at risk. The Children of Israel welcomed and respected his high moral character and position and regarded him as a teacher who contributed to the development of human character.

The Prophet Mohammed never insisted that Jews or Christians should convert to Islam. Mohammad merely gently propagated his mission. Nevertheless, in the biography of the Prophet Mohammed, and other books on the history of Islam, some prominent converts to Islam from both Judaism and Christianity are mentioned.

In summary, the Prophet Mohammed, although always following the commands of the Almighty God, was very kindly disposed towards the Children of Israel and accorded them full freedom to carry out their religious duties according to Mosaic law.

The Attitude of the Jews Towards Mohammed

Most foreign historians and researches believe that in view of the positive attitude expressed in verses about the Children of Israel before Hejira (Mecci Verses) the Prophet Mohammed was under the impression that the Children of Israel would soon and easily convert to Islam.

Historians have unfortunately treated this subject incorrectly. The best grounds for thinking that the Prophet Mohammed did not hold such a view is to be found in the approving verses about the Children of Israel and the *Holy Torah*, and the exhortations to peaceful co-existence with followers of religions with a heavenly book found there. During the prophet's lifetime no religious wars took place involving the Children of Israel and Moslems. The Prophet Mohammed endeavoured all his life to disseminate Islam among the atheists, and to remove the obstacles created by unbelievers, Khavaredge, atheists, and also some members of his own family who opposed him. No evidence concerning conflicts with the Children of Israel on religious subjects is mentioned in the *Gracious Koran* or in history books.

During the Khandagh War, the Jews, in accordance with the Constitutional Law of Medina, joined the Prophet Mohammed's army to fight the polytheists. The Prophet surmised that the Jews might leave him at the beginning of the war, and that they would join the army of Mecca. On Saturday 15th of Shaval in the year 3 of the Hijera, Abdalla Ibn Obi with his army corps and a group of people (the Munafiqun) split off from the army of Islam, abandoning the Moslems and the Jews. Despite rumours of the Jews intending to join the army of Mecca, they in fact stayed at the side of the Moslems. The Prophet

Mohammed sent the Jews who were fighting with him to their homes on Saturday as a mark of respect for the Holy day of the Jews.

Another instance is the Khaybar Conquest. It was agreed that those who would not be able to go would stay and continue their daily work. After the conquest of Khaybar by the capable commander Imam Ali, the law of temporary marriage to the Jewish slaves was exceptionally cancelled. The Prophet Mohammed forbade the Moslem soldiers to enter the gardens and palm plantations of the Jews. He even married a Jewish woman called Safia (daughter of Hoyyah).

The Speech of the Prophet Mohammed at the Last Hajj Ceremony

The Prophet Mohammed in his last Hajj ceremony, which was called *Hajj Al-Veda*, addressed the crowd and said: 'Oh people! Your God is one, your ancestor is the same (Adam), you are the children of Adam and are made from soil, so your main material is soil. No one of you is superior to another, but in the view of the Almighty God, one who is virtuous and afraid of God is superior'.

Constitutional Law of Islam

The agreement between the Prophet Mohammed and the Jews of Medina is considered to be the Constitutional Law of Islam. According to some scholars it is the first codified constitutional law in the world. I refer briefly to the emigration of the Prophet Mohammed from Mecca to Medina accompanied by Moslems, and also to the conclusion of the agreement. After the mosque in Medina had been built and Moslems brought their wives from Mecca to Medina, the Prophet Mohammed promulgated a constitutional law for Medina, which was an independent city. This Constitutional Law consists of fifty-two Articles and was drafted by the prophet himself; unlike the verses of the *Gracious Koran*, it was not the fruit of divine inspiration. Of the fifty-two Articles, twenty-five are relevant to Moslems, and twenty-five to the followers of other faiths.

The Medina Constitutional Law was designed in such a way as to enable the followers of different faiths to live in the city together, and to carry out their religious duties and observances without being disturbed by the others. This law was promulgated in the first year of the Hejira, that is 623 C.E. (one year after the emigration of the prophet from Mecca to Medina).

In accordance with the Constitutional Law, each resident of Medina was permitted to maintain his religion and to carry out his religious duties in safety and without interference or objections by others. The followers of all faiths had to take part in the defense of the city if Yasreb (Medina) was attacked.

Here are some Articles of the Constitutional Law of the Prophet

CHAPTER TWELVE

Mohammed. It must be said that the idea of ensuring freedom of worship for the followers of other religions in Medina had its roots in the *Gracious Koran*. Let us again look at verse *62* of the *Sura Al-Baqara*h:

> Surely those who believe, and those who are Jews, and the Christians, and the Sabians, whoever believes in Allah and the Last day and does good, they shall have their reward from their Lord, and there is no fear for them, nor shall they grieve.
>
> إِنَّ الَّذِينَ آمَنُوا وَالَّذِينَ هَادُوا وَالنَّصَارَى وَالصَّابِئِينَ مَنْ آمَنَ بِاللَّهِ وَالْيَوْمِ الْآخِرِ وَعَمِلَ صَالِحًا فَلَهُمْ أَجْرُهُمْ عِندَ رَبِّهِمْ وَلَا خَوْفٌ عَلَيْهِمْ وَلَا هُمْ يَحْزَنُونَ ۝

This demonstrates that the Almighty God did not deprive the Jews, Christians and even Sabians, of his mercy, provided that they were real believers and engaged in doing good deeds.

The Almighty God in *Sura Al-Maidah 66* says the following about Jews and Christians:

> And if they had kept up the Tavrat and the Injeel and that which was revealed to them from their Lord, they would certainly have eaten from above them and from beneath their feet; there is a party of them keeping to the moderate course, and (as for) most of them, evil is that which they do.
>
> وَلَوْ أَنَّهُمْ أَقَامُوا التَّوْرَاةَ وَالْإِنجِيلَ وَمَا أُنزِلَ إِلَيْهِم مِّن رَّبِّهِمْ لَأَكَلُوا مِن فَوْقِهِمْ وَمِن تَحْتِ أَرْجُلِهِم مِّنْهُمْ أُمَّةٌ مُّقْتَصِدَةٌ وَكَثِيرٌ مِّنْهُمْ سَاءَ مَا يَعْمَلُونَ

At the time of the Prophet Mohammed and the first four caliphs, the followers of religions with a Holy Book were able to lead pleasant and relaxed lives, especially in the Hijaz. But at the time of Omavian, the life of the Jews became problematical owing to different views being held by various groups of Moslems. This lead to the disappearance of the Jews, after they had played such an important role in the development of the Hijaz, including the founding of villages and small towns. The antagonism displayed against the Jews was in fact in contrast with the principles of Islam, a religion that called for support of, and friendly relations with, the followers of religions with a Holy Book.

The Prophet Mohammed felt compelled to wipe out some tribes that might have blocked the expansion of Islam, and among these there were also some Jewish tribes. Thereafter, the Prophet Mohammed concluded agreements with the Jews in Kheybar, in accordance with which they were permitted to engage in agriculture and other work. He never exerted any pressure on them in matters connected with their religion. The trusted slave of Khadijeh, who was a Jew and had served in the house of the Prophet Mohammed, moved with Fatima to the house of Ali. According to Khadijeh, the Prophet had told this slave that religion was devoid of force, and that he would not be subjected to pressure to convert to Islam. The Jews never placed any obstacles in the path of the Prophet or his followers. They accepted that his prophetic mission was directed at idol worshippers and polytheists. It must again be emphasized that the Children of Israel did not, at any time, cause trouble for the Moslems of Medina.

We can obtain valuable information on the personality of the Prophet Mohammed and his attitude to non-Moslems through studying both the *Gracious Koran* and Jewish history. The Prophet had an attractive and interesting character. He was famous for his honesty and truthfulness, attributes that caused people to call him 'Mohammed the Trustworthy'. Mohammed's character and personal reputation greatly facilitated the carrying out of his mission. He was a young man who thought deeply, and among other things often took the initiative in helping the oppressed. In associating himself with an agreement against oppression and tyranny, Mohammed demonstrated his spiritual qualities even before he began his mission.

It is clear that the Jews in Hijaz were glad to have the Prophet Mohammed in their midst, and supported him; the reason was that they sympathized with his call to idol worshippers and atheists, including oppressors and plunderers, to join Monotheism. Moreover, they endorsed his ethical and religious values, as well as his concepts of honour.

At that time, the Prophet Mohammed was shunned and ridiculed even by his uncle Abul Habb and his wife (the sister of Abu-Sofeyan). The Moslems were surrounded in the Abutaleb Mountains for three years, even after the change of Kibbla, and the gates of Mecca were closed to the Prophet and his followers.

After the Prophet had arrived at Medina, the people decided to accept his rule because he belonged to the famous Ghoraysh tribe, but above all because he had an exemplary character and was the symbol of purity, truthfulness and honour. The Jews, who did not accept anybody but the Almighty God, preferred as their ruler someone who was also the propagator of a monotheistic religion, rather than someone like Abdallah Ibn Abi (the head of Munafiqun), who made an attempt to usurp power.

Chronology of the Prophet's life and events at the beginning of Islam after the Common Era (C.E.)

570	Year of birth of the Prophet Mohammed
610	Year of the beginning of Call
620	Mohammed's reputed 'Night Journey' from Mecca to Jerusalem and thence to the Seventh Heaven.
622	Mohammed's Hejira from Mecca to Medina (The beginning of the history of Islam)
624	Change of Kibbla from Jerusalem to Kabba
630	Conquest of Mecca

CHAPTER TWELVE

632-634	Abu-Bakr Caliphate
634-644	Omar Caliphate
635	Conquest of Damascus
637	Moslem Rule in Jerusalem and Tisfoon (under Omar)
641	Conquest of Iran and Egypt
641	Foundation of Cairo
642	Foundation of Amro Mosque in Cairo
657-661	Caliphate of Ali Ibn Abi Taleb
661-680	Caliphate of Moaviah Ibn Abi Sofian
661-750	Caliphate of Omavid in Damascus
680	Martyrdom of Imam Hossein Ibn Ali in Kaarbala
683-684	Caliphate of Moaviah the Second
685-705	Caliphate of Abd Al-Malek Marvan
691-694	Foundation of Al-Aqsa Mosque and building of Ghobat-Assokhra in Jerusalem
693-862	Moslem Rule in Armenia
705-725	Caliphate of Waled the First
705	Foundation of Great Mosque in Damascus
715-717	Caliphate of Soleiman Ibn Abdol-Malek

Jerusalem was in the hands of the Egyptian Kingdom until 878 C.E. In 1099 C.E., the Christians conquered the city and massacred the Moslem and Jews there. Jerusalem was under Ottoman rule from 1517 until 1918. In 1920 the city was placed under the British Mandate, and in the year 1948, the Government of Israel was established.

Studying Both the *Gracious Koran* and Jewish History

The Prophet had an attractive and interesting character. He was famous for his honesty and truthfulness, attributes that caused people to call him 'Mohammed the Trustworthy.' Mohammed's character and personal reputation greatly facilitated the carrying out of his mission. He was a young man who thought deeply, and among other things often took the initiative in helping the oppressed. In associating himself with an agreement against oppression and tyranny, Mohammed demonstrated his spiritual qualities even before his mission.

It is clear that the Jews in Hijaz were glad to have the Prophet Mohammed in their midst, and supported him; the reason was that they sympathized with his call to idol worshippers and atheists, including oppressors and plunderers, to join monotheism. Moreover, they endorsed his ethical and religious values, as well as his concepts of honour.

At that time the Prophet Mohammed was shunned and ridiculed even by his uncle Abu-Laveb and his wife (the sister of Abu-Sofeyan). The reason Moslems were surrounded in the Abutaleb Mountains for three years, even after the change of Kibbla, and the gates of Mecca were closed to the Prophet and his followers.

Chapter Thirteen

•

The Prophet Jesus Christ

In his book, *Jesus, The Messenger of Islam*, Dr. Ahmad Beheshti describes how the Romans conquered the country of the Jews and subjugated them. Their cruel and dictatorial regime not only tortured the Prophet Jesus, who had only twelve disciples, but they persecuted countless others, including scientists and sages, such as Rabbi Akiba who was a teacher revered by hundreds of pupils. The Romans skinned him alive. Their persecution of the Jews was designed to induce them to cease worshipping the sole Almighty God and to adore instead the Roman idols. The Romans used to torture the Jews for entertainment (as they did others), suggesting that they call upon their God to deliver them from the harm inflicted upon them. (The incident of Jewish sages and scientists being put to death has rarely been mentioned in Jewish literature, and hardly ever in non-Jewish literature).

Unfortunately, later the Christianized Romans tried to blame the Children of Israel for crucifying Jesus, exonerating themselves. (*Jesus, the Messenger of Islam* p56.) Regrettably, many Christians have repeated this version of events during history, although in reality Christianity is but a branch of Judaism. Although the three great Popes of Catholicism affirmed repeatedly to their worldwide flock that the Children of Israel were innocent of the killing of the Prophet Jesus, and stressed that it is not equitable to blame the Jews today for what happened at the time of their ancestors, yet to this day there are still groups, mostly primitive and uneducated, who maintain the ancient falsehoods and inflict suffering on the Jews, the latest major manifestation of this being the Holocaust, orchestrated by Adolf Hitler.

Among the many accusations levelled against the Children of Israel over the years one often repeated story concerns the killing, at Passover time, of Christian boys in order to use their blood in the preparation of the unleavened bread eaten by Jews on the occasion of that feast. The absurdity of this tale is paramount when compared, first with the fact that in the Jewish religion blood is considered unclean, especially human blood, and hence it is forbidden to mingle blood with food; secondly, there is the express prohibition against murder in the Ten Commandments. Received by the Prophet Moses by the Almighty God. In the Middle Ages, when plagues and infectious diseases were rampant and thousands died as a result, the Jews were often accused of having poisoned the wells by sorcery. They were blamed for causing disease, because the incidence of death among the Jews from these maladies was low due to the fact that, according to their religious precepts, they had to keep themselves clean and thus avoid infection.

The Prophet Jesus Christ

Other wrongful accusations against the Jews were contained in the infamous *Protocols of the Elders of Zion*, a faked document produced about one hundred years ago and widely distributed in Europe; after having been translated into many languages. Although the falseness of this paper was proved, and enlightened people rejected it categorically, there were always ignorant groups who used it to castigate the Jews.

Unfortunately, these false assertions of dangerous Jewish activities spread to the Islamic countries and provided the motives for massacres of Jews in many cities. In the year 1840, the rulers of the Ottoman Empire forbade the spreading of the Passover story of the use of blood in preparing unleavened bread, but it nevertheless is still given credence in less developed countries.

In the end, the Roman Empire was defeated by monotheism, which is today accepted as the only form of religion by over two billion people in the world. Many of these do not know that Christianity sprang from Judaism, and that the Prophet Jesus and his apostles and pupils were Jews. It is natural that despite worshipping a single God, the religion originated by Jesus had to include the time and life situation. This factor of time and place usually has an influence on religions. We see that even in Christianity there has been some splitting into different branches. It must be mentioned here that during the last fifteen years, due to the endeavours of John Paul II, there has been a noticeably better understanding between Jews and the world of Christianity.

I wish that this humanistic movement should continue and lead to permanent peace among human beings, especially in the Islamic countries, between the followers of Judaism, Christianity and Islam, on the basis of *Sura Al-Imran 64* (see below).

The Unification of Monotheistics

The *Gracious Koran* considers the followers of religions that have a heavenly book as being equally worthy, and recommends to them to emphasize what is common in their beliefs, and to stand united against atheism and polytheism.

Say: O followers of the Book! come to an equitable proposition between us and you that we shall not serve any but Allah and (that) we shall not associate aught with Him, and (that) some of us shall not take others for lords besides Allah; but if they turn back, then say: Bear witness that we are Muslims.

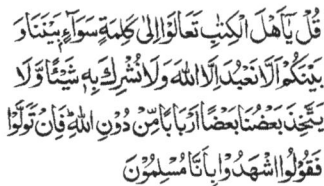

Al-Imran 64

Unfortunately there are some misunderstandings in the history of Christianity. Since the Prophet Jesus and his disciples were of Jewish origin, they were hated by the Romans – who were idolaters – because of the Jewish belief in one Almighty God; a hatred which finally led to the biggest tragedy in Jewish history.

Thank God that the cruel superpower, the Roman Empire, was ultimately defeated by monotheism, and all its glory, idols and temples vanished from the world. Thereafter monotheism spread all over Europe and eventually the world.

How Christianity Spread

Many historians have studied the history of the Children of Israel after the destruction of the Temple, and the Jewish state then in existence, by the Romans. Two Jews whose mother tongue was Greek and who were familiar with the traditions and cultures of the Greeks, other Europeans and the Asian peoples, tried to persuade idol worshippers to adopt Christianity. To reach this aim they transformed one of the Jewish sects into an independent religion. One of these men was St. Paul and the other was Joses Barnabas (A Christian missionary and companion of Paul. *Acts 4:36*).

The Jews, who were scattered over different parts of the world, were important factors in spreading monotheism and combating idolatry. Dr. Habib Levy in his history book writes as follows:

> The Romans, especially Pontius Pilate, were fully aware of the beliefs of the Jews about the advent and rise of the Messiah. They knew that when the Messiah will come the enemies of the Children of Israel would be defeated and their country would become independent. The Great Cyrus, who defeated the Chaldeans who had been the enemies of the Jews, was named as 'Messiah' by the Prophet Isaiah.

The teachings of the Prophet Jesus were not tending to violence, but rather called upon the believers to have patience and strong faith, yet the Romans, and especially Pilate, were not familiar with these ideas. Pilate thought he could eliminate the Messiah, the deliverer of the Jewish nation, thereby adding to the pride and success of the Roman Empire. The Christian religious leaders pretended that Pilate was innocent of such designs. However, the way the Roman soldiers treated the Prophet Jesus, their glee at his suffering, reflected their own and their master's attitude. There is no doubt that such a terrible thing as the crucifixion could not have happened without the approval and planning of the Romans, especially Pontius Pilate, the dictator of Judea.

Christians do believe that the Gospels were written a few centuries after the time of the Prophet Jesus, and that they were partly based on hearsay handed down from one generation to the next. It is clear that the Gospels were written under Greek and Roman influences. These societies were inimical to the Jews and hence they attributed the fault for the persecution and death of Jesus Christ to the Jews rather than to the Romans.

About the Prophet Jesus

Jerusalem passed from hand to hand. As the Jews were skillful in neither administration, government nor politics, the Greek ruler of Egypt succeeded in taking over the city. To better entrench their rule they caused many of the Jewish residents of Jerusalem to move to Egypt, thus creating the greatest concentration of Jews at Alexandria. There the Jews were in close touch with Greek civilization, and the holy books were translated from Hebrew into Greek. Jerusalem being a far-away colony for Egypt's Ptolemaic rulers, the latter did not interfere with life there – provided their taxes were paid.

In the year 198 C.E., Jerusalem was taken over by the descendants of Seleucus I, one of the marshals of Alexander the Great who ruled from Antioch. Being thus nearer to Jerusalem they took a closer interest in events there and enforced the imposed penetration of Hellenic culture, thus clashing with the orthodox Jewish circles. This development reached its zenith at the time of Epiphanes Antiochus, who made the mistake of putting a statue of Zeus in the Temple of Solomon. This lead to the outbreak of a rebellion, lead by the Hasmonean family, which became known as the Maccabee Revolt. The rebels succeeded in driving the Greeks out of Jerusalem and rebuilt the temple, which had been violated and profaned. The new Maccabee rulers were both religious leaders and politicians. They insisted on strict adherence to the law, and the people began to yearn for the more liberal times when strangers had governed them.

The Birth of Jesus and the New Uprising

It was in this period that Jesus was born. The Romans repeated the mistake of earlier rulers by affixing a statue of a golden eagle above the Temple gate. This action infuriated the Jews and led to an uprising. It was led by two members of the Maccabee group, who decided to destroy the statue. The Romans regarded this not only as a rebellion, but also as an insult to their religion, and reacted strongly. After much blood had been spilt the rebellion was defeated and the two Maccabeans were burnt at the stake. A few years later, there was another uprising against the Romans, and more than two thousand Jews were hanged.

Chapter Fourteen

•

The Imams and the Jews

Imam Ali and the Jews

When Imam Ali heard that a Moslem Arab had pulled an ankle ring off the foot of a Jewish woman he was so angry that he shouted, 'If Moslems die today they will deserve it.' One of the best proofs of the kindness of Imam Ali towards the Jews is the interpretation of the *Sura Daher 7-9* written by the Shiite and Sunnite interpreters.

Antar, the Faithful Slave of the Prophet's Family*

Due to the animosity of the atheists, the Prophet Mohammed had to take refuge for three years in his uncle's house located in a valley in the Abu Taleb Mountains. During this period, Imam Ali supplied food for Khadijeh, the faithful wife of the Prophet, with the help of Antar, her freed slave. Antar, out of appreciation for the kindness of the Prophet Mohammed and his wife, used to prepare food for them in violation of the economic restrictions in force in the Ghoraysh tribe against Moslems. In the book, *Ayesha After the Prophet*, written by the German writer Frischler and translated by Zabihallah Mansouri, the following story appears, a story that clearly shows that Antar, who faithfully served Khadijeh and later Fatima Zahra to the end of his life, ignored the boycott imposed by Mecca against Moslems.

> One day Khadijeh, the prophet's wife, called me and said, 'Antar! We have to stay here because we are Moslems and are forbidden to return to Mecca; if we go there we will be killed, because the Ghoryash tribe believe that it is lawful to shed the blood of Moslems. But you are not a Moslem, you can return to Mecca. So I will set you free, and thus you will be able to return to Mecca. You may serve one of the nobles there, and not suffer from hunger, as we do here.' I answered that, although there is not enough food here I do not really suffer from hunger, but even if I did I would not complain because you have treated me well and although I was your slave you did not behave as if you were the master. I have had a good life in your house since the beginning, I will not complain and I will not leave. Khadijeh said, 'But we

* Some say his real name was Anbar

do not know for how long we will be in this situation, and I am not sure when we will leave here.' I replied, 'As I told you before, I will stay with you as long as you will be here and suffer deprivations, because I cannot abandon your daughter Fatima. I am going to serve her as long as I live because I have got used to serving her.' Khadijeh said, 'Oh Antar! Now that you like my daughter so much, why do you not convert to Islam?' I answered, 'We Jews keep our faith' – and I asked – 'will you force me to convert?' She responded, 'I will never force you to convert because the Prophet held that no one should be forced to change his faith, that is something done only voluntarily.'

Om Kolhoum and Fatima used to help their mother. Although Fatima was physically weak, she nevertheless bore her share of the fatigues of daily life. The stores of food we had brought from Mecca were exhausted and hunger began to be felt. By chance, a caravan passed the valley on its way to Mecca. We asked Ataba, the caravan leader to sell us food, and he agreed in order to repay Abu Taleb's kindness to him.

Although Ataba was aware of the fact that we were hungry and really needed food, he did not demand exorbitant sums. He sold us all the food he had and our men carried it to the valley. Some other caravans were passing near the valley, but none of them agreed to sell us anything.

After he reached Mecca, Ataba Ibn Rabia was condemned by the leaders of the Ghoryash tribe for selling goods to us. However, he pretended not to have known about the order forbidding commerce with us and convinced them that he had sold us the goods because we paid an exceptionally good price.

Chapter Fifteen

Imam Ali's Justice

Dr. Habib Levy, the author of a history of the Iranian Jews, has devoted a short chapter to the life of the Imam Ali and his wise speeches. *Nahj-Al-Balagheh of Imam Ali* is a collection of his thoughts, a wealth of wisdom, honour and humanity.

I quote a passage from Dr. Levy's book:

> Moavieh, son of Abu Sofyan, was the commander in the Ohod War against the Prophet, but later converted to Islam.
>
> The opponents of the Caliph set out for Basra. Imam Ali also set out for Basra in order to prevent war. Finally, the Jamal War broke out among the Moslems. The Caliph, after conquering Basra, departed for Kuffa and chose it as his caliphate centre.
>
> In 647 C.E. the Saffein War broke out between the Caliph and Moavieh. Following a suggestion made by Amro As to Moavieh, the soldiers of Syria each raised a volume of the *Koran* on their spears and demanded that the *Gracious Koran* should be the referee between them. It was a clever trick. If the demand were refused, the Caliph's soldiers would escape. The Caliph as arbitrator chose Abu Mussa, and Moavieh was – unjustly – proclaimed to be the Caliph. Following this there were differences of opinion between the followers of Imam Ali, which included Khvaredge (outsiders) who were against the caliphs.
>
> Khariat, one of the Arab leaders, incited Iranians, Kurds and Christians against Imam Ali, and this led to a great uprising. In 660 (40th year of the Hejira) Imam Ali made peace with Moavieh, but in 661 Ibn Moljem, who was one of the Khavaredge, martyred him.

So as to convey to the reader the striking personality, kindness and profound thoughts of Ali Ibn Abi-Taleb, as well as the wise speeches of Imam Ali, I will cite here some parts of the *Nahj-Al-Balagheh*.

> According to the Prophet, those will be saved whose hands are not stained with the blood of the oppressed, and whose tongue is not defiled by curses against the wealth and honour of people.
>
> A leader who oppresses those he leads is the worst kind of person.
>
> In the eye of the Almighty God, intimates and strangers are the same.

The world is the cradle of love and kindness. The world is the school of perfection and ethics.

The Almighty God prefers a slave who is kinder, friendlier and more sincere and loves him more than He does others. Such a person does not cheat or accuse people, and does not give preference to wealth over spiritual values. He abhors those who misuse religion for profane purposes.

A cruel man imagines himself to be free and thinks that God is not aware of his misdeeds. He will continue to wallow in sin and debauchery until the flames of God's anger will burn him.

Oh, thou humans that consider yourselves superior to animals. If eating and sleeping is all you seek from life then you are baser than animals.

Oh, thou humans that look down on brute beasts, if your life is but filled with animal-like deeds, are you any better?

Jealousy destroys faith.

Never pass a night devoured by feelings of spite and hostility, and never be malevolent.

Be righteous in order not to fall.

The following is part of a directive to Mohammed Ibn Abi Bakr:

Oh Mohammed! Continue to administer justice until the last minute of your life and do not rue the time devoted to justice, because in our government nothing is dearer than justice.

As part of his instructions to Malek Ashtar he writes:

Oh Malek! There is nothing better to take with you to the other world than good deeds. Oh victor! Oh hero! You may fight anyone but the Almighty God.

Never think that because you are doing your duty you are excused. Do not blindly obey every order given to you, and do not expect that any order you give will be obeyed blindly.

Oppressors are the enemy of God.

CHAPTER FIFTEEN

Imam Jaafar Sadegh and Problem Solving

Iranian Jews believe that Imam Jaafar Sadegh invited the Jews of Medina to the wedding ceremony of his son Imam Moussa Kazem. He showed them great kindness and hospitality. Obviously, the support given by the founder of the Shiite faith to religious minorities demonstrates that Islam advocates dignity, kindness and the observation of human rights.

The following article published by *Shofar*, a Jewish magazine in New York, shows how Imam Jafaar Sadegh succeeded in terminating the harassment of the Jews by some Moslems who did not follow the injunctions of the *Gracious Koran*:

> Imam Jaafar Sadegh is one of the outstanding and high-ranking Imams of Islam. He had a rare talent for leadership and was very wise, being also an excellent speaker. He customarily extended his protection to Jews who were being subjected to persecution and harassment by bigots.

In the past there were some periods during which such torments of the Jews were routine. Non-Moslems did not have civil and human rights, these being reserved for Moslems. The Jews being in a minority, they had no option but to submit and bear their suffering, and this grew worse with the passage of time. The Jews were even forced against their will to admit some of their persecutors to their festivities, and Jewish girls were often married to Moslems by force, contrary to the will of the families. There were no authorities that were prepared to intervene and help them because the interests of the Moslems always predominated. In this situation the Jews, having consulted amongst themselves, decided to appeal to the Imam Jaafar Sadegh for help.

The Imam acceded to the pleadings of the Jews, and determined to put an end to the prevailing situation. He asked the representative of the Jews to come back to him a few days later.

Imam Jaafar knew that the problem could only be solved through religion. When the representative of the Jews again stood before him and respectfully kissed his hands, the wise Imam permitted him to sit. The Jew was on tenterhooks, not knowing whether to expect good news or bad. Finally the Imam said to him: 'From now on, no Moslem will hurt the Jews.' The messenger wept with joy and, thanking the Imam, left to bring the glad tidings to the Jewish community.

In a famous sermon that the Imam delivered the next day in the presence of a great number of Moslems he said:

> It is clear that the followers of Islam and the path of the Prophet are pure, clean, and beloved of God. However, I was informed that a group of deviants and sinners have violated this purity, and have

aroused the anger of Almighty God by socializing with the Jews. They have eaten with them and even slept with them. Woe to all of us if this be true, because these people have disgraced our religion and have called curses and impurity down upon us, whereas the Jews remain pure and will be saved in Heaven. These people deserve Hell, not only for themselves but also for their children and children's children. So all of you, after today's ablution and prayer, should repent before Almighty God, and should promise not to repeat such deeds; only thus can you obtain forgiveness and put an end to your misfortune. Thus the conclusion for you is that you must stay away from the Jews as much as possible and abstain from contact with them.

The wise speech of the Imam put an end to the harassment and persecution of the Jews. The latter respected and appreciated him more than ever before.

The period of disaster for the Jews was thus at an end, but instead they had acquired – quite wrongly – the reputation of being impure so that no one should touch them or their food. And this was done to the Jews whom the Prophet Mohammed had called 'The People that has a heavenly book'.

Chapter Sixteen

•

Why does Anti-Semitism Exist?

Anti-Semitism is not a problem within the Children of Israel. It exists due to the ignorance and lack of knowledge of people who seek relief from their wild and cruel inner hostility by wreaking it on the Jews. It is a regrettable phenomenon.

The long-term hostility of the atheist Roman Empire (which lasted quite a few centuries) against the Jews and monotheism motivated many wars and rebellions. Owing to the poisonous attitude of the powerful Roman government against monotheism, as a result of which people became afraid of the Almighty God, a wave of unreasonable hatred against the Jews swept though various groups of ignorant and illiterate people of the time. The situation became so serious that cruelty and tyranny towards Jews, and indeed the killing of Jews, became an everyday event and was actually considered a good and necessary deed.

By the will of Almighty God, the Roman government and its idols vanished; however, victorious Christianity – initially considered as being a Europeanized branch of Judaism – did not manage, or indeed set out, to vanquish the hatred and opposition against Jews. This attitude had a lasting effect. Even today the democratic and humanistic principles enshrined in the great philosophies, which do not differentiate between people on the basis of religion, are still unknown to most people, and many, because they believe in untrue and unjust slanders, still consider the Jews to have negative attributes.

Anti-Semitism According to the Vews of Jean-Paul Sartre

In the past, governments that faced problems often sought scapegoats that could be blamed in order to escape criticism themselves. Naturally, the Jews, who, as minorities everywhere, were always in weak positions and were frequently the victims of the governments' manoeuvres.

Sartre, the French philosopher, in his book on Anti-Semitism, carried out a study from the social and psychological points of view. He came to the conclusion that human beings always stood in need of someone, be it groups or nations, who could be blamed for their own mistakes and misfortunes. In the course of history, the Jews many times filled this role. In the course of his analysis, he shows that Jews, whether as individuals or as a nation, do not have any innate characteristics that would justify the hostility shown towards them. He concludes that their problem was, and is, that they are strangers and submissive. Sartre is convinced that those who show hostility towards the Jews are in fact suffering from mental illness, and their place should be in hospital – not society. He believed the patience and stability of the Jewish nation, when faced with hardship and persecution, exacerbates the hatred and spitefulness of its enemies. These find themselves ranged against a nation that firmly stands by its values and moral standards, depriving them of the satisfaction that should be derived from their expressions of hostility. Among the reasons for the glory of the Jewish nation over the centuries are found in their humanity, patience, hopefulness, resort to Divine mercy, and belief in the peaceful future of the human race.

The History of Anti-Semitism

The Children of Israel are the oldest monotheists, who have managed to survive despite oppression, massacres and other agonies. After having lost their independence following the Roman conquest of their country they, being mostly a minority in countries of homogenous strangers, have been subjected almost everywhere to persecution on the part of the rulers, particularly if these were atheists. Anti-Semitism began to exist after the Roman conquests of most of the Middle East, including the land of Canaan, and this resulted in cruel Roman emperors becoming rulers of the Children of Israel. The Romans displayed great hostility towards all the foreign peoples under their sway, and especially against those who adhered to different religions. One of their hobbies was, for instance, to torture a Jew and to ask him to call upon his God to save him so that they, the Romans, could see what their God looked like. The Romans used to install idols in the Jews' holiest places, and demanded that they prostrate themselves before the idols. In the end, however, it was the glorious Roman Empire, with all its temples and idols that was defeated by Monotheism.

It was difficult for the Romans to accept their defeat, and in order to take revenge they decided to blame the Children of Israel for the crucifixion of the Prophet Jesus. If one considers the strong hostility displayed by Pontius Pilate towards the Jews and the continuous pressure on them that he exercised for them to abandon monotheism and revert to the installation of idols in their temple, then it becomes clear that the Roman proconsul did not have to ask permission of the Children of Israel for the crucifixion of the Prophet Jesus. However, even if the story that he did indeed ask the elders of the Jews in Jerusalem for their agreement to the crucifixion is true, this merely shows that there was a small group of Jews that was servile to Romans and did not hesitate to betray their people, most of whom at the time regarded Jesus as the Messiah.

Most of the sages of Christianity in the initial period were Jews. They did not lose their hope in the appearance of the Messiah despite the long periods of suppression. At that time the crucifixion of the prophet Jesus, who had twelve disciples, was not the only event of this kind. Numerous Jewish sages, such as Rabbi Akiba, who had hundreds of pupils, were savagely killed by the Romans without their having asked the permission of the Children of Israel or their elders.

The Prophet Jesus, although known as the founder of Christianity, was born and died as a Jew. It is usual that when a new religion or doctrine makes its appearance and gradually gains ground, its exponents deny the previously reigning religion or doctrine by all means at their disposal. Anti-Semitism can be studied in tens of books written on the subject. Briefly, it can be said that lack of knowledge of human relations, shallow judgment and prejudice may cause a person, or a nation, to be judged contrary to reason and justice. The last four Popes have emphasized the innocence of the Children of Israel crucifying the Prophet Jesus, and, in their daily prayers, ask the Almighty God to forgive them for the oppression of the Children of Israel over the centuries.

There can be no doubt that among the Children of Israel, as among any people, there are good and bad persons. The point to be emphasized, however, is that since the Prophet Moses led the people of Israel to the land of Canaan no religious wars were initiated by the Jews; the principal reason for this is to be found in the fact that Jews do not engage in missionary activity for the purpose of converting the followers of other religions.

It cannot be denied that the Jews have for long suffered persecution merely because they were Jews. It is interesting to note that there are some anti-Semites who do not know why they are hostile to Jews. The Jewish nation has always tried to avoid killing, has abstained from religious wars, and has, wherever they went, been part of the progressive forces that brought development and welfare to the people around them.

Yet the Jews, uniquely, are always expected to behave fairly and well, and all of them are considered blameworthy if any one of them deviates from the path of virtue. To hold in contempt a nation, almost half of which consists of university graduates, is simply not fair.

Anti-Semitism is Not Fair

A. The Children of Israel were the first monotheists in the world. This nation has never initiated wars against other countries, nations or religions.

B. According to the principles of Judaism, human beings are, without exception, Holy, created by the Almighty God, and carry the light of the Creator.

C. The Children of Israel pray for the health, welfare and blessing of all human beings in their prayers, and believe that the faithful followers of all religions will be saved.

D. The Children of Israel are not hostile to any nation, and every Jew is commanded to love others as much as he does himself.

E. The contributions to science by the Jews are so outstanding that they should change anti-Semitic tendencies of any person who is aware of these contributions.

F. The Children of Israel are, and have been so since the time of the Prophet Moses, kind to strangers, following the biblical commandment which orders them not to forget the strangers, because they themselves had been strangers in Egypt. This is in contrast to what happens in many countries where equality for strangers is no more than a dream.

Anti-Semitism is not an exclusive characteristic of ignorant people – there are educated people who subscribe to such views, who take rumours as facts, and fail to explore the subject in depth. Perhaps not everyone knows that human civilization is indebted to two Jews for some of its basic tenets: to the Prophet Moses for monotheism and law, and to the Prophet Jesus for the code of ethics. It should also not be forgotten that the Light of the East, the Prophet Mohammed whose ancestors sprang from the same source as those of the Children of Israel, was the saver of millions of atheists and idol worshippers.

Anti-Semitism is the Result of Prejudice and Lack of Knowledge

This being so, it can be hoped that in the future improvements in education and the dissemination of knowledge will cure this evil to some extent. Beyond this, however, the phenomenon will disappear once people respect each other and a feeling of brotherhood and unity becomes more widespread.

Two personal memories:

1. In Zurich, Switzerland, there are beautiful and well-appointed houses whose Jewish owners and inhabitants, old and young, were all burnt at the stake some years ago, allegedly for the greater glory of the Almighty God and the Prophet Jesus. In modern times these attitudes have changed – even a President of Switzerland can be Jewish (Mrs. Dreyfus). The Jewish residents of the country are highly respected, and pictures of notable Jews who have contributed to the

welfare of the country are displayed in schoolbooks. As a mark of respect towards the Jewish community the government of Switzerland has rebuilt synagogues that were destroyed in the past, even in cities that today have no Jewish residents.

2. When I was a boy I used to live in Anglalaj Place, Tabriz, Iran, and our house was adjacent to an Armenian church, surrounded by high walls. The day after the anniversary of the crucifixion of the Prophet Jesus, when we woke up in the morning we saw that our yard was full of stones thrown, 1,900 years after the event, at our house as revenge for His crucifixion! The broken windows were fixed by order of the police, but nobody apologized to us. Comparing that event to the history of the past, I thought to myself: would Pilate, the haughty Roman enemy of the Jews, really have asked their permission to crucify the Prophet Jesus? This story surely cannot be true. Its existence can only be due to lack of correct information. The Armenians do not, of course, engage in such behaviour anywhere today, because concepts and behaviours have changed, and that is in fact a sign of hope for a better future. I would not omit to say that my best friends were Armenian, and I will never forget them.

Failure of the Children of Israel to Explain Themselves

The leader of a powerful and influential tribe invites some of the The Children of Israel to his house for a meal. He is unaware of the religious laws regarding slaughter and food (Kashrut) and prepares a royal table of delicacies. After inviting the guests to eat he finds, to his surprise, that they ignore his invitation and refrain from eating. In answer to the host's question the Jews declare that they are forbidden by their religion to eat non-kosher food at any time and anywhere, even in the house of their brother. The leader of the tribe thinks that the guests consider them and their food unclean. By failing to explain beforehand the limitations placed upon them by their religious food laws, the Jewish guests contributed to the dissemination of the seeds of anti-Semitism. This could have been avoided if they had acted in time to explain, and at the same time making clear that in Judaism, no one is unclean. In the *Holy Torah*, and also in the *Gracious Koran*, Almighty God tells his faithful that all human beings have been graced with His soul and light. To consider someone as impure is a great sin. It means regarding God's light and soul as impure.

The Author's Suggestion

The dust of the past should be wiped away, and the road to understanding should be paved. Every sane and decent man, no matter what his religion is, should combat racism, oppression, corruption and discrimination. For monotheists, whether they be Moslems, Jews or Christians, fighting the mentioned phenomena is a Divine duty. Jews should show that despite their sufferings they have remained peaceful, kind and appreciative of human values. In order to eliminate the problem of anti-Semitism intellectuals of different religions should discern the causes of the malady and eradicate them. To achieve this, clear thinking, bravery and adherence to spiritual values is always necessary.

Chapter Seventeen

•

The Children of Israel Represent a Benefit for All Religions

Since the beginning of history, Judaism was never a threat to Islam, Islamic or non-Islamic countries in any way, and there is no reason to suppose this fact will change. There is no reason for the Jews to ever be a threat:

1. Judaism is not a religion that proselytizes. The Jews do not try to encourage non-Jews to convert to Judaism, bar in particular cases, such as a marriage between an adherent of the Jewish faith and a person embracing another religion. In such cases, great effort is required of the person seeking to convert, and not everyone is capable of doing this. During the fifty-odd years Israel's existence, I have never heard of a Moslem converting to Judaism. Jews always honour the followers of other faiths.

2. According to the Jewish faith it is forbidden to dominate or oppress believers of other religions. It is not permitted to own the property of other people unless it has been paid for (remember the purchase of land by Ibrahim for his wife's grave).The Jewish nation has never initiated a war for reasons of religion, and will never do so in the future. It is against its religious law. Matters pertaining to the State of Israel are seen as local, political subjects – not religious ones. Its very foundation was motivated by the wish to provide a haven from persecution and oppression.

3. Since the time of the Prophet Mohammed, no Moslem was killed by Jews except in the event of war against Jewish sinners in the Hijaz after God had sent down verses to his true prophet. This subject is quite clear in the Islamic interpretations and historical books. No Moslem martyr is mentioned in the history of these wars. The Jews, who believed in Mohammed as a prophet, and who took into consideration the holy *Suras* of *Al-Anam 55-57*, *Ibrahim 4-5*, *Al-Imran 164*, *Yunus 47*, *Al-Nahl 93* and *Al-Jummah 2* in which it is mentioned that the prophetic mission of Mohammed was merely to save the idolaters, surrendered themselves to him almost without a fight. The verses emphasize clearly that the Jews and Christians were free to follow their own religions and were not to be forced to convert to Islam.

4. Judaism does not differentiate between Jews and non-Jews. Both

the *Holy Torah* and the *Koran* state that human beings carry the soul of the Almighty God, and thus all human beings are holy. Above all, the Bible demands strictly that one should love one's fellow creatures.

5. The number of followers of Islam in the world is over 1.5 billion, whereas there are about 15 million Jews in the world, i.e. the followers of Islam are a hundred times more numerous than the Jews. Considering this proportion, is it not natural that such a small minority, being also intellectually inclined and wise, should seek to have friendly and peaceful relations with other monotheistic peoples?

6. The problems between Israel and the Arabs will eventually be resolved and peace will prevail, if the countries whose financial advantages are involved in the dispute will give them a chance to end their hostility. It is encouraging to see that the level of culture of the Jews and Arabs is improving, and little by little they will find out that peace is the best way of solving problems, and that the secret of a calm and happy life for their peoples lies in peace and co-existence.

7. Jews have lived all over the world – from Spain and Morocco to Indonesia and China – but they have never indulged in activities such as betrayal, disobedience or killing.

8. Jews have always been patriotic in every country they lived in. They try hard to contribute to the development of the country in which they live, to create wealth and promote science and industry. During the 1,400 years history of Islam we do not see any negative point about the Jews.

9. Judaism is not a proselytizing religion. As Jews do not try to expand their faith, they do not have, and never have had, disputes with the followers of other religions.

The followers of Judaism respect the ideas of the believers of other religions. Jews believe that God loves all of his creatures, especially those who do good deeds. In Judaism, the philosophy of creation lies in doing good deeds. The Prophet Moses always considered all human beings as being the creatures of God, and thus having the right to live. He never denied this right to anybody.

The secret of Judaism's long existence is to be found in the idea that *other people are also part of creation* and deserve respect and consideration. Unfortunately, a few persons like Nazim, Baruch Goldstein, Yigal Amir, and

CHAPTER SEVENTEEN

their friends as well as a Russian lady who, having recently insulted Moslem religious susceptibilities, is added to this black list, have ruined not only their own lives, but also caused their nation to have a bad reputation. Murder and Judaism do not go hand in hand.

Jews, as the believers in a heavenly religion and as the Chosen People, have had to undertake great responsibilities, the most important of which is to prevail upon other people to do good deeds. The word chosen must not be interpreted as meaning 'the best'; it means, simply, that the Jews have been chosen to disseminate monotheism. They were the first to introduce, into a world of idols and idolatry, the notion of a single God whose theme is goodness and good deeds. The *Psalms*, the *Torah*, and some other books of the Bible, which have been written by Jews, bear witness to this fact. It is interesting, in retrospect, to note that a small, simple, nation not outstanding in economics, science or military might, succeeded in the great task of converting the world, as it was then, from adoring and fearing idols to the monotheistic idea.

The Litany of Jewish Prayer

The Jewish prayer represents the connection between the human beings and God. It contains supplications to God to grant guidance for doing good deeds, and for abstaining from sin; God is asked to provide his blessings for the Children of Israel and for everybody else. The synagogue is the House of God, and it is for all the nations of the world. Words to that effect are inscribed above the entrance of every synagogue in the world.

The Prophet Moses and the Ten Commandments

The Prophet Moses, the founder of Judaism, the divine and civil lawgiver of all adherents of monotheistic religions, is loved not only by the Jews, but praised also by all other monotheists, especially the Moslems. In the *Holy Koran* the name of Moses is referred to with obvious dignity and respect. The name of this hero of the history of humanity – the symbol of freedom and the standard-bearer in the struggle against idolatry and pharaonic oppression – is mentioned one hundred and twenty-six times in the *Holy Koran*. In it, the Prophet occupies a high and indeed unique position not comparable to that of anybody else in any holy book. Moses, as a fighter against tyranny and injustice, is known as the symbol of freedom and the leader in the struggle for deliverance. He is also acclaimed as an example of leadership for other prophets and is seen as one of the great freedom fighters of history.

It is not easy to know Moses, the only prophet who spoke face to face with God. No chapter or book can be adequate to describe him. His splendour is beyond words.

Moses brought God's Ten Commandments not only for the Jews, but also for the well being of every human being. As it is impossible to introduce this great man of God in my book, I only mention here the eternal Ten Commandments which mankind will observe forever.

The Ten Commandments

1. I am the Lord your God, who brought you out of the land of Egypt.

2. You shall not make for yourself an idol.

3. You shall not take the name of the Lord your God in vain.

4. Remember the Sabbath day, to keep it holy.

5. Honour your father and your mother .

6. You shall not murder.

7. You shall not commit adultery.

8. You shall not steal.

9. You shall not bear false witness against your neighbour.

10. You shall not covet your neighbour's house; you shall not covet your neighbour's wife or his male servant or his female servant or his ox or his donkey or anything that belongs to your neighbour.

Final Reflections

The writer has tried to express his ideas about the importance of understanding and friendship among the followers of monotheistic religions according to his beliefs and not on the basis of politics or the taste of politicians.

Today, the peoples of the world have opened a new page in their social life. They are tired of anger, coarseness, war and destruction, and think of a just peace and friendship as their ultimate aim.

Religion is supposed to teach honour, morals, dignity, forgiveness and courage to human beings. Otherwise what is the benefit it confers?

The heavenly religions recommend durable, comprehensive and just peace for human beings. Peaceful co-existence is one of the teachings and yearnings of Ibrahimian religions.

Chapter Seventeen

At the end of my book I would like to emphasize that God has sent his prophets in order to lead human beings to safe, peaceful life far from hostility, fear and poverty.

Islam is the religion of peace and inner serenity, and submission to the will of God. In the Hebrew language, the word *Shalom* – which means peace, inner serenity, health and relaxation of the mind – is used more than any word (as is the word *Salam* which is mentioned in the *Holy Koran*). Thus tormenting, bothering, subjugating and causing impoverishment of God's slaves are in fact a sacrilege and an insult to God's will. I hereby advise the Jews (my fellow believers) to keep behaving respectfully towards other peoples, especially the followers of monotheistic religions (Christians, Moslems and Zoroastrians). I also recommend to my co-religionists to follow the precepts of the *Torah* and not to sacrifice purity, justice and faith for the sake of politics at any time anywhere.

I ask all Moslems and all Christians to adopt a more positive view about their Jewish fellow human beings, not to generalize, and not to judge them because of their ancestors' sins, and to try and establish a just and durable peace under which the rights of all parties are treated with equity and consideration. Let us pray together that God will help us to be pure, to do good, and to follow the teachings of his prophets.

BIBLIOGRAPHY

•

The *Holy Koran*
The *Holy Torah*
The *New Testament*

The *Gracious Koran*
Translated and interpreted by Baha Eddin Khorramshahi

Nahj-Al-Balagheh
By Imam Ali

Jesus: The Messenger of Islam
Dr. Ahmad Beheshti

Protocols of the Elders of Zion

Ayesha after the Prophet
By Frischler & Translated by Zabihallah Mansouri

Jews of Iran
By Dr. Habib Levy

Anti-Semitism
Jean-Paul Sartre

ABOUT THE AUTHOR

•

Youssef Khakshouri

Youssef Khakshouri was born in Rezaieh (Orumia), West Azerbaijam, Iran. He finished his schooling at the only high school in the city, but was unable to continue on to a university because of World War II. Instead, young and inexperienced though he was, he entered business, which took him as far as Tabriz and Tehran. In 1952 he traveled to Germany to establish a business importing dried fruits from Iran. His hard work and good products made him a successful businessman. His family joined him about a year later. Eventually they immigrated to Switzerland and lived in Zurich for twenty-three years. They had to emigrate again when, as a result of the Islamic Revolution in Iran, all their portable and fixed assets were confiscated and they could no longer afford to reside in Switzerland. The Khakshouris decided to live in Israel, and have a comfortable life there.

He feels privileged to enjoy the friendship of good, honest, sincere and religious Moslem people, especially among his former classmates. He has kept in contact with his Moslem friends in Germany, Switzerland, and Iran. 'I have traveled to many places and have met many people,' says Mr. Khakshouri, 'but my best and most sincere three friends were Moslems who encouraged me to be the author of this book. May their souls be blessed.'

Mr. Khakshouri is a gentle, kind, humble and wise man who has extended considerable help to others and made significant contributions to the development of culture and humanity. He hopes that this book will pave the way to friendship and brotherhood between the followers of different religions and will help more people to look realistically at their own and others' religions.

Verse 10, Sura Chambers

The believers are a band of brothers.
Make peace among your brothers and fear god,
so that you may be shown mercy.

اِنَّمَا الْمُؤْمِنُونَ اِخْوَةٌ فَاَصْلِحُوا بَیْنَ اِخْوَیْکُمْ وَ اتَّقُوا اللّٰهَ لَعَلَّکُمْ تُرْحَمُونَ

سوره الحجرات آیه ۱۰

جز این نیست که مؤمنان (به خدا) برادرند
پس اصلاح کنید میان برادران و پرهیزگار باشید
تا مورد رحمتِ خداوند متعال قرار گیرید

The above verse was written and presented to me by
the late Mr Harichi, an honest Moslem and
one of the people who encouraged me
to write this book.

It is published here in honour of his eternal memory.

First published in Great Britain by

Elliott & Thompson Ltd
27 John Street
London WC1N 2BX

© Youssef Khakshouri 2006

The right of Youssef Khakshouri to be identified as the
author of this work has been asserted by him
in accordance with the Copyright Designs
and Patents Act 1988.

No part of this publication may be reproduced, stored
in a retrieval system or transmitted, in any form
or by any means, electronic, mechanical,
photocopying, recording or otherwise,
without the prior permission
of the publisher.

ISBN 1 904027 44 X

First edition

Printed and bound in Malta by Progress Press